To my father,
Harry Sunderland,
my first pastor
and mentor

ACKNOWLEDGMENTS

The ideas and images that coalesced to form the basis of *Getting Through Grief* evolved during the past twenty-six years. The formative process of membership in the Association for Clinical Pastoral Education (ACPE) throughout this period has been a rich blessing. The clinical pastoral education movement surrounded me with peers in clinical supervision and provided me with an educational model that bore fruit in the "Equipping Laypeople for Ministry" (ELM) program. I have been privileged to share ELM workshops with ACPE supervisors and lay and ordained pastoral ministers across the United States. Thanks are due to ACPE supervisors and pastors who share my vision and to hundreds of lay pastors who have shared their ministries with me. From them I have learned much of what I know about ministry.

A generous contribution to this project was made by Bill Barrett and Jim Proctor of the Corporate Communications Department of Service Corporation International Inc., (SCI) who invited me to prepare the script from which the SCI video, "Working Through Your Grief," was developed.

Thanks are due to Samuel Southard and Walter Brueggemann, who reviewed the first draft of this text, reminded me that theological pursuit of my topic must be explicate rather than implicit, and suggested directions that search might take.

A special contribution was made to this project by Earl Shelp, my friend and colleague for the past fifteen years. Our co-editorship of a series of books in Theology and Ministry, and more recently our joint

Acknowledgments

effort in ministry and authorship relating to the Church and AIDS, have enriched me and contributed greatly to my learning and my ministry. The "Care Team" concept of congregational pastoral care to families facing catastrophic illnesses or disabilities, which developed out of our AIDS ministries in Houston, will have a creative impact on the future shape and direction of pastoral care in the congregation.

Most of all, thanks are due to my wife, Noel, and Dion, Brent, Quentin, Granger, and their families. My family has provided me with a safe and strong place where I have learned to love and to be loved. Here, most of all, I have learned that "growing through grief" is not just a catchy phrase, but a lifelong process that is both a challenge and a goal toward which to strive. Their love makes that effort possible and the goal attainable.

CONTENTS

INTRODUCTION

A man can die but once: we owe God a death.
KING HENRY IV II.III.ii. 249

When Sorrows Come . . .

The week of October 14, 1991, began like any other week. On Monday morning I delivered my weekly grief psychology lecture to thirty students planning to take up careers in funeral homes—and be more aware of their opportunities to assist individuals and families to struggle through funerals and their ensuing experiences of mourning. Thence to the airport and a flight to St. Louis to present a seminar to community caregivers whose professional lives placed them in contact with children in grief. My attention was caught by a headline on the front page of the morning's *New York Times:* "Washington Voters Weigh if There Is a Right to Die." I turned to the novel I was currently reading, Colleen McCullough's *The Grass Crown,* and found my place:

"How long has my daughter got?"
"We don't know. The doctors think very little time now, but she's fighting it. Yet she has some great fear, too. I don't know what, or why. Romans are not afraid of dying."
"Or so we tell ourselves, Marcus Livius. But beneath the show of fearlessness, there's always the terror of the unknown."
"Death isn't an unknown."
"Do you not think so? Perhaps it's rather that life is sweet."
"Sometimes."[1]

9

Later, in another setting, McCullough describes a father's grief as he sits beside the body of his son, dead at the age of eleven:

> The grief, the loss, the finality of it all sat within him like a huge lead boulder. . . . There before him lay the ruin of his house, there lay all that was left of his dearest friend, the companion of his old age, the heir to his name, his fortune, his reputation, his public career. Vanished in the space of thirty hours. . . . The cold had worsened, the lungs had become inflamed, and the heart squeezed dry of animation. The story of a thousand illnesses. No one's fault, no one's design. . . . For those left behind, knowing all, feeling all, it was the prelude to an emptiness in the midst of life that would not cease until life was over. His son was dead. His friend was gone forever.[2]

Writing to a friend about his son's death, Lucius Cornelius Sulla reflected:

> My son was infinitely precious. From the first time I saw him, a naked laughing tot in the nursery, I loved him with all my heart. In him, I found the perfect companion. No matter what I did, he thought it a wonder. . . . And then he died. So suddenly, so unexpectedly! If one could but have time. . . . Yet what preparation can a father make for the death of his son? . . . I am missing a part of the core of myself, there is an emptiness that can never be filled.[3]

That evening in my hotel room, I enjoyed a few minutes with the cast of "Cheers." To the dismay of his colleagues in the bar, Woody had befriended an older, recently widowed woman. They dated briefly, and in the closing scene, she thanked him for giving her back some of the joy she missed after her husband's death. Turning to CBS's "Northern Exposure," I found that Maggie had become convinced that a stray dog she had befriended was really Rick, her erstwhile live-in boy friend who had died in a previous episode. Challenged by another of the show's characters, Dr. Fleischman, to give up her fantasy, Maggie responded: "Maybe you're right! . . . Maybe I did have some leftover things to work out about Rick, and maybe I did work them out with a dog! But so what?"

October 15 entailed TV and radio interviews associated with the Grief Seminar, in which the special needs of bereaved children were reviewed in brief news segments. The seminar followed on October 16, to more than four hundred caregivers, some sharing their own stories of children's grief. I flew home via Shreveport, where two nights earlier, a random, senseless, drive-by shooting had led to the death of an innocent bystander, to the news of the country's worst shooting massacre, with twenty-two patrons shot dead in a restaurant in Killeen, Texas.

So, life goes on. Some griefs affect a few individuals, a family—some an entire community, a state, even the nation. We manage to laugh sometimes in the midst of our grief but mostly we cry. After horrors like that in Killeen, we are stunned into speechless shock, unable to comprehend the depth of such a tragedy. Yet, except for the people of Killeen, we have already relegated that tragedy to memory and the history books.

Human preoccupation with dying and death has been an abiding ∟ theme from the earliest development of human consciousness. The pyramids are monumental reminders of that obsession in ancient Egypt. Egyptologists suggest that the pharaohs were preoccupied for much of their lives with dying and the afterlife. Burial sites and customs are one of the most prolific sources of knowledge of ancient cultures, a fact attested to by the attention given to new archaeological digs that uncover glimpses of how people lived, the ways they dealt with the mystery of death, and the fascination that assumptions of existence beyond death held for the living.

The literary sources of many cultures pause in their historical accounts to record the death of leaders and the circumstances and locations of their burial. Genesis closes the account of the life of Sarah (Gen. 23:19), then that of Abraham: "Abraham . . . died in a good old age, an old man and full of years, and was gathered to his people. His sons Isaac and Ishmael buried him in the cave of Machpelah, in the field of Ephron son of Zohar the Hittite, east of Mamre, the field that Abraham purchased from the Hittites. There Abraham was buried, with his wife Sarah" (25:8-10).

Funerals and the mourning practices they usher in tend to become more elaborate with the stature of the deceased, as illustrated in the deaths of sovereigns or American presidents. The death and burial sites of the great and famous have held endless fascination for succeeding generations, illustrated, for example, by tourists' pilgrimages to the graves of notables in English cathedrals or country churchyards. Nor is it surprising, with the emergence of the social sciences, that dying, death, and the grief they evoke should become ✕ not only subjects in the fields of art, poetry, and music but of psychology and sociology. Few human events have received the attention accorded to death and bereavement or have been studied with the thoroughness to which the grief process has been subjected during the past thirty years.[4] Yet while investigation of the psychology and sociology of dying and death has continued since the early 1900s, only since 1960 has widespread public attention been given to understanding the impact of "the grief process" on the human psyche.

In 1979, Michael Simpson retorted that "death is a very badly kept secret: such an unmentionable and taboo topic that there are more than 750 books in print asserting that we are ignoring the subject."[5] Updating his introductory remarks in his 1987 edition, he adds that there is something bizarre about the fact that there are now thousands of books in which the issue of death as a taboo topic is discussed.

Dying and death have been discussed by theologians since the Church Fathers, but, as in the area of psychosocial research, the literature has received little attention other than from theological and research colleagues. There is now a flood of research into the impact on grief on personal and family lives. The recently published *Dictionary of Pastoral Care and Counseling* provides an extensive review of the pastoral-care literature relative to ministry to the bereaved.

In this context, since pastoral care of the dying and the bereaved has been characteristic of the church since the first century, it is all the more baffling and disturbing to discover that gaps exist between understanding the grief process and the provision of effective pastoral support of people in mourning, or of effective all-age grief-education programs. That such gaps do exist is borne out both by discussions with parish pastors and priests who have been frank in acknowledging the little time they are able to give to support of members in grief, and the comments of congregants who express the deepest concern—often the sense of betrayal—that they felt abandoned by their communities of faith following the deaths of family members. It seems that, for all the books and articles on dying, death, and grief, and the many opportunities for clergy to attend continuing-education seminars on these topics, few congregations have instituted comprehensive grief-support and education programs.

Hence, another book on dying, death, and grief: *Getting Through Grief* is an effort to resolve a problem area created by the apparent failure in many congregations to provide effective grief education and to set it in the context of compassionate pastoral care of mourners. It addresses specifically the tasks that face Christian congregations as their members fulfill their commitment to bear one another's burdens of grief, and so fulfill the law of Christ.

Chapter 1 examines the universality of the grief experience and surveys the development of efforts to analyze and understand grief and its processes, beginning with Freud, Klein, and Lindemann. It suggests that pastoral theologians were late on the scene, but, beginning with the work of Edgar Jackson in the 1950s, have been engaged in attempts to identify and delineate the implications for pastoral theology and the practice of emerging psychological insights into the nature of the grief process. The chapter introduces the perception that clergy grief seminars have yet to bear fruit in adequate care of bereaved congregants.

The second chapter proposes that the customary format for understanding the grief process—identification of the so-called stages of grief—is being superseded by a return to an earlier concept—namely, the *work* of grieving, or more definitively, recognizing and completing the *tasks* of mourning. First adopted by Sigmund Freud and continued by Erich Lindemann, this model has been enlarged in scope by William Worden.[6] It is somewhat expanded here into a new conceptualization, replacing the previous stereotype of a rigid, linear grief process. This more dynamic process is helpful in identifying the points at which mourners may be "blocked" in their ability to work through their grief experiences, and the point at which the mourner is better able to break out of the cycle of grief, assume new tasks, and enter new relationships.

Chapter 3 examines the nature and scope of grief as a human experience, which is far more pervasive in human life than bereavement, the term we apply to grief evoked by death of a loved one or close friend. By the 1950s, and with growing emphasis in the 1970s, psychologists and sociologists recognized that grief is a normal response to any experience of loss or change. Two important conclusions are drawn: First, since loss and change are endemic in each life, we are continuously thrust into and emerge from grief; second, grief episodes can "pile up." The struggle to work through and complete the tasks of mourning may be complicated by the failure of grieving people to recognize and acknowledge other unresolved griefs due to loss or change. Thus, bereavement may result in grief of unbearable intensity. Similarly, lack of awareness of other sources of grief on the part of caregivers may result in less effective support to mourners by their communities, including their congregations.

A comprehensive congregational grief-support ministry is developed in chapter 4, using the fictitious case study of Mary and John

Gibson. It includes making a survey of needs of grieving congregants, recording appropriate family data, recruiting laypeople to provide continuing support throughout families' periods of mourning, and the need to pay particular attention to children in grief—the congregation's "forgotten mourners." First Church's ministry to Mary and her family following John Gibson's death suggests how these steps may lead to a comprehensive program designed to meet the needs of a family in grief. Attention is also focused on understanding and responding to the needs of grieving children.

The congregation's ministry to bereaved members is further elaborated in chapter 5, which examines the special needs evoked by grief due to trauma—for example, murder, suicide, and the deaths of children, including grief evoked by Sudden Infant Death Syndrome. Grief ministry must be formed in response to the individual needs of members and their families, as well as to the cause and circumstances of the loved one's death. The chapter describes how support groups can be developed in congregations, using trained and supervised lay caregivers. Such groups are important adjuncts to individual care, because grief, while in some sense private, is also communal. Participation in the socialization process, facilitated by a support group, is often instrumental in assisting mourners to work through grief and begin the process of reconstructing life without the loved one.

Key aspects that need careful planning prior to implementing a grief support group are identified—for example, whether the group is "open" or "closed," continuous or time-limited; the selection, training, and supervision of group facilitators; and the establishment of guidelines for group facilitators; and the establishment of guidelines for group structures and procedures. This process is illustrated by the use one couple made of their participation in a support group.

The relationship between pastoral support of bereaved individuals and families, and the inclusion of grief education in the congregation's programs, is addressed in chapter 6. The development of a comprehensive grief-education program is a necessary corollary to the establishing of grief ministry. The opportunity for grief education is inherent in every act of the congregation's grief ministry. Jane's support of Mary Gibson becomes an opportunity for Mary (and Jane) to continue learning about bereavement and how to fashion and receive grief support. At least some part of every grief-support group session or visit, for example, has either an implicit or explicit learning potential. Jane's visits with Mary also create the possibility for Mary to understand the extent of the griefs she is experiencing, her need to work through not only John's death, but the earlier bankruptcy, moving, her daughter's divorce, and any other losses or changes that have intensified her bereavement. Had Mary been aware before John's death of the nature and extent of grief, she might have been better able to complete the tasks of morning, at least with a greater sense of awareness and confidence that it is work that can be seen through to completion. She might have faced a lesser risk of becoming deeply depressed.

When grief *education* programs incorporate a *pastoral* intent and consequence, pastoral ministry to a grief-stricken family is offered in the context of learning to which each member of the family has already been exposed. Grief education is best begun in early childhood and much can and should be accomplished within the family. Congregations can assist by making provision for parental education; inclusion of the grief process in the church-school curriculum will help and reassure children and parents alike. Parents can be assisted to understand the nature of grief, how grief education can be undertaken and the tasks of mourning faced in the family, based on the special needs of children at their respective stages of development and readiness. Questions discussed include the wisdom of involving children in planning family funerals and memorial services.

Society appears to be emerging from the long period in which these issues were not discussed in families or communities. Failure to address these concerns has left gaps in the preparation to face dying and death in every generation, which must now be addressed. The religious community, through the agency of the local congregation, should be in the forefront of these efforts.

In addition to outlining the areas I have addressed, it is as well to identify the book's limits. The original outline of *Getting Through Grief* included three chapters that addressed theological issues— theologies of death, the theological structure and intent of funeral liturgies, and the meaning of the funeral and mourning rituals for the congregation as a community of faith. In the interests of keeping this book to a reasonable length, I have passed over these aspects of grief and plan to address them in a second volume. They deserve and need more attention than was possible here. In any case, my primary goal was the exploration of the nature and quality of congregations' ministries to people in mourning, and of their grief-education opportunities in light of some of these concerns. I hope to have contributed to consciousness-raising in this area, and to have identified what I see as the urgent need for further dialogue, both as to theologies of death and issues of praxis. For the moment, praxis in the form of pastoral care of the bereaved holds the attention. If, as I believe, congregations in general have yet to give adequate attention to these matters, it is time to address them and to invite further discussion of both the theology and practice of the church's ministry to the bereaved.

Finally, a word about definitions. Following general usage, I use the term *grief* to refer to the psychological process of adjustment to *any* substantive loss or change—substantive, that is, to the grieving person. *Grieving* refers to the individual's experience of the loss or life-change. *Bereavement* refers to the particular grief that accompanies and is evoked by the death of a loved one. *Mourning* refers to the more or less institutionalized process followed by survivors as they adapt to the death of loved ones. However, the term may be applied more generally to adjustment to the everyday losses and changes that belong to the human condition. That is, adjustment to loss and resolution of grief will be factors of the degree to which a person is able to complete the tasks of *mourning.*

CHAPTER 1

Understanding Grief

I cannot but remember such things were,
That were most precious to me.
                                    MACBETH IV.iii.222

Grief in Literature and the Arts

On occasions during radio or TV interviews when introduced as a "grief expert," I usually respond that there are no grief *experts*. Unless, of course, one includes every individual who has more or less effectively completed the task of mourning the death of a loved one. For we all respond to our personal griefs in our individual ways. The form taken by grief in each person is determined by a variety of factors which will be addressed in this volume. Suffice it to say here that, while bereaved people may be guided and helped by others, each must be responsible for determining how he or she will face and master the hard work of mourning. We are challenged, in that sense, to become our own "experts" in grieving.

If, indeed, there are those who may be termed "grief experts," they are as likely to be found as much among artists, poets, and dramatists scattered throughout the pages of history as in the ranks of today's social scientists. Read again, for example, Psalm 6:6-7:

> I am weary with my moaning;
>   every night I flood my bed with tears;
> I drench my couch with my weeping.
> My eyes waste away because of grief;
>   they grow weak because of all my woes.

Or Psalm 13:1-2*a*:

> How long, O Lᴏʀᴅ? Will you forget me forever?
> How long will you hide your face from me?
> How long must I bear pain in my soul,
> and have sorrow in my heart all day long?

The fragile nature of human existence was addressed by the Roman poet Juvenal (c. 60–130): "Death alone reveals how small are men's poor bodies."[1] A century earlier, Virgil also had written about the impact of grief in human life. By the Middle Ages, grief was a frequent topic for poets and dramatists. Sir Fulke Greville, an attendant of Elizabeth I, noted that "silence augmenteth grief,"[2] and Samuel Johnson later attributed to Richard Hooker (1554–1600) an aspect of grief work that social scientists were to rediscover in the twentieth century: "Change is not made without inconvenience, even from worse to better."[3]

But it was William Shakespeare who most poignantly depicted grief and its anguish. Not surprisingly, he addressed grief with both humor and the intensity of tragedy. In *Much Ado About Nothing*, Don Pedro's conversation with a group of friends is interrupted by Benedick:

> **Benedick:** I have the toothache.
>
> **Don Pedro:** Draw it.
>
> **Benedick:** Hang it!
>
> **Claudio:** You must hang it first, and draw it afterwards.
>
> **Don Pedro:** What? Sigh for the toothache?
>
> **Leon:** Where is but a humor or a worm.
>
> **Benedick:** *Well, everyone can master a grief but he that has it.*
> *Much Ado About Nothing* III.ii.28
> (emphasis added)

In a similar humorous vein, while discussing the ensuing battle, Falstaff is acutely aware of its dangers and asks Prince Hal not to leave him on the battlefield if he is injured, but to dispatch him with his sword:

> **Falstaff:** Hal, if thou see me down in the battle and bestride me, so; 'tis a point of friendship.
>
> **Prince:** Nothing but a colossus can do thee that friendship. Say thy prayers, and farewell.

Falstaff: I would 'twere bed-time, Hal, and all well.

Prince: Why, thou owest God a death. *(Exit)*

Falstaff: 'Tis not due yet; I would be loath to pay him before his day. What need I be so forward with him that calls not on me?

King Henry IV I.V.i.121ff.

Shakespeare also reminds us of the inevitability of death in II *King Henry IV*. Feeble, a soldier, is ordered by Bardolph to stand aside on threat of death. He responds:

Feeble: By my troth, I care not; a man can die but once: we owe God a death: I'll ne'er bear a base mind: an't be my destiny, so; an't be not, so: no man is too good to serve's prince; and let it go which way it will, he that dies this year is quit for the next.

King Henry IV II.III.ii.249ff.

Shakespeare's art is most intense in the tragedies. In *Hamlet*, King Claudius observes the grief-stricken Ophelia and grieves over her state:

King: O, this is the poison of deep grief; it springs
All from her father's death.
O Gertrude, Gertrude,
When sorrows come, they come not single spies,
But in battalions. First, her father slain:
Next, your son gone.

Hamlet IV.v.78ff. (emphasis added)

The Earl of Gloucester, in *King Lear*, informs his son, Edgar, that the insane king's life is in danger; the Duke of Cornwall and Lear's daughters, Regan and Goneril, seek to destroy Lear in order to consolidate their power. Plans are made to save Lear's life, and Edgar is left in soliloquy:

When we our betters see bearing our woes,
We scarcely think our miseries our foes.
Who alone suffers suffers most i' the mind,
Leaving free things and happy shows behind:
But then the mind much sufferance doth o'erskip,
When grief hath mates, and bearing fellowship.
How light and portable my pain seems now,
When that which makes me bend makes the king bow.

King Lear III.vi.109ff.

The same light is displayed dramatically in *Macbeth*. Following Macbeth's assumption of the throne after King Duncan's murder, the king's son, Malcolm, together with other loyalists, makes plans to overthrow Macbeth. As they plan the final battle, word is brought that Macbeth's soldiers have killed Macduff's family. Macduff, shocked by the news, withdraws from the group, but is challenged by Malcolm:

> **Malcolm:**   What, man! ne'er pull your hat upon your brows;
> Give sorrow words: the grief that does not speak
> Whispers the o'er-fraught heart and bids it break.

Then Malcolm overlooks entirely the deepest reaches of Macduff's grief:

> **Malcolm:**   Be comforted:
> Let's make us medicines of our great revenge,
> To cure this deadly grief.
>
> **Macduff:**   *(mutters to himself)*
> He has no children. . . .
>
> **Malcolm:**   Dispute it like a man.
>
> **Macduff:**   I shall do so;
> But I must also feel it as a man:
> I cannot but remember such things were,
> That were most precious to me.
>   *Macbeth* IV.iii.208ff.

The nineteenth-century poet Robert Southey also knew how bystanders so easily gloss over the anguish of the bereaved:

> Thou has been call'd, O Sleep, the friend of Woe,
> But 'tis the happy who have called thee so.[4]

Poets and dramatists knew not only that death or anticipation of death evoked the deepest levels of grief, but that other losses also were accompanied by grief. For example, W. E. Aytoun, a contemporary of Robert Southey, expressed another dimension of grief:

> They bore within their breasts the grief
> That fame can never heal
> The deep, unutterable woe
> Which none but exiles know.[5]

But it is the grief that we know as bereavement to which authors have most frequently and movingly attended. Annie Dillard, whose prose is laced through and through by her poetry, is a contemporary writer who notes the fragility of our human lives, so threatened by death. Dillard notes that "in the open, anything might happen:"

> Dorothy Dunnett, the great medievalist, states categorically: "There is no reply, in clear terrain, to an archer in cover." Any copperhead anywhere is an archer in cover; how much more so is God! Invisibility is the all-time great "cover"; and that the one infinite power deals so extravagantly and unfathomably in death—death morning, noon, and night, all manner of death—makes that power an archer, there is no getting around it. And we the people are so vulnerable. Our bodies are shot with mortality. Our legs are fear and our arms are time.[6]

To the insights of poets and dramatists are added those of other artists. Who can be unmoved by the anguish of Michaelangelo's *Pieta,* or Josef Israel's painting of a peasant sitting by the bed on which his wife lies dead?[7] One of the most moving musical expressions of grief comes from one of the nation's newest and most gifted composers, John Corigliano. His first major work, *Symphony No. 1,* was composed following the death of a close friend, and dedicated to him. It is an eloquent expression of grief's deepest anguish and stands alongside Berlioz's *Symphonie Fantastique,* or the heartbreak expressed in the aria "Ahime'! Dove trascorsi?" from Gluck's *Orfeo ed Euridice,* in which Orfeo grieves Euridice's death:

> What shall I do without Eurydice?
> Where shall I go without my love?
> . . . .
> Oh, let my suffering cease for ever with my life.

Leo Tolstoy's *The Death of Ivan Ilych* remains one of the most moving portrayals of the theme of death, encompassing denial, fear, and grief, and the preoccupation with death that often accompanies a chronic illness:

> How it happened it is impossible to say because it came about step by step, unnoticed, but in the third month of Ivan Ilych's illness, his wife, his daughter, his son, his acquaintances, the doctors, the servants and above all himself, were aware that the whole interest he had for other people were whether he would vacate his place, and at last release the living room from the discomfort caused by his presence and be himself released from his sufferings.[8]

On Researching Grief

When one turns from the arts to the social sciences, one moves from the attempt to represent grief in art, music, poetry, and drama to twentieth-century efforts to analyze "the grief process." Throughout human existence, dying, death, and the rituals associated with bereavement have occupied individuals and entire cultures.[9] Yet it was not until the twentieth century, with the advent of the social sciences, particularly clinical psychology and psychoanalytic theory, that *research* into the etiology and nature of grief began. This was an important and necessary step toward understanding the nature of grief and its impact on the lives of individuals, although, as we will see, that step has not necessarily led to more effective support to the person in grief. Yet the pace of this research was slow, and until the 1950s was largely limited to a few psychoanalysts.

Sigmund Freud was one of the first researchers to identify unresolved grief as one source of immobilizing depression. Freud discussed the *work* of mourning, and pointed out that the testing of reality is an essential part of that work: "Reality-testing has shown that the loved object no longer exists, and the ego proceeds to demand that all libido shall be withdrawn from its attachments to that object. This demand arouses understandable opposition, [which] can be so intense that a turning away from reality takes place."[10]

Freud believed that for people in what came to be identified as "normal grief," "respect for reality gains the day." His preliminary investigation led him to ask why this process of carrying out the behest of reality bit by bit, "which is in the nature of a compromise, should be so extraordinarily painful?"[11] He added that it was not even known "by what economic measures the work of mourning is carried through." He conjectured that

> reality passes its verdict—that the object no longer exists—upon each single one of the memories and hopes through which the libido was attached to the lost object, and the ego, confronted as it were with the decision whether it will share this fate, is persuaded by the sum of narcissistic satisfactions in being alive to sever its attachment to the non-existent object. We may imagine that, because of the slowness and the gradual way in which this severance is achieved, the expenditure of energy necessary for it becomes somehow dissipated by the time the task is carried through.[12]

Freud's investigations were extended by other psychoanalysts, notably Melanie Klein. Interest was focused on the reaction of the grieving person to separation from the loved one. Unfortunately, in one sense, "normal" mourning was being viewed only from the perspective of psychoanalytical theory, which continued to shape almost all early efforts to understand human grief:

> In normal mourning early psychotic anxieties are reactivated; the mourner is in fact ill, but, because this state of mind is so common and seems so natural to us, we do not call mourning an illness. . . . To put my conclusions more precisely: I should say that in mourning the subject goes through a modified and transitory manic-depressive state and overcomes it, thus repeating, though in different circumstances and with different manifestations, the processes which the child normally goes through in his early development. [13]

Klein suggested that the pining which accompanies normal mourning is marked by a dependence "which becomes an incentive to reparation and preservation of the [lost] object." This dependence is creative because it is dominated by love, in contrast to a dependence based on hatred for the loved one who has died. Thus, in intense grief, "The love for the object wells up and the mourner feels more strongly that life inside and outside will go on after all, and that the lost loved object can be preserved within." Suffering can then become productive, even bringing out quite new gifts in some people, who may turn to painting, writing, or other productive activities as they experience the stress of frustrations and hardships. Others may become more capable of appreciating people and things, more tolerant in their relations with others. As Klein notes, "they become wiser." [14]

During the early 1940s, Erich Lindemann, a psychoanalyst and Psychiatrist-in-Chief at Massachusetts General Hospital, took research into the grief process a stage further. He began to investigate the relationship between acute grief and various psychosomatic illnesses. In his classic essay published in 1944, [15] Lindemann suggested that acute grief seems to be not a medical or psychiatric disorder, but a normal reaction to a distressing situation. He noted, however, that bereavement—that is, the sudden cessation of social interaction, is of special interest because it is often cited among the alleged psychogenic factors in psychosomatic disorders. Lindemann attributed his interest in this research to the recognition that, in a population of 41 patients with ulcerative colitis, 33 developed their disease in close time-relationship to the loss of an important person. "Indeed, it was this observation which first gave impetus for detailed study of grief." [16] When asked to comment on his findings, he stated that the essential emotion in cases of ulcerative colitis is sorrow.[17] His paper elaborated the following points:

1. Acute grief is a definite syndrome with psychological and somatic manifestations.
2. This syndrome may appear immediately after a crisis; it may be delayed, exaggerated, or apparently absent.
3. In place of the typical syndrome there may be distorted pictures, each of which represents one special aspect of the grief syndrome.
4. Through counseling, these distorted pictures can be successfully transformed into a normal grief reaction with resolution.[18]

In his study of "normal grief," Lindemann identified a variety of symptoms of grief in its acute stage: sensations of somatic distress occurring in waves that last from twenty minutes to one hour, a feeling of tightness in the throat, shortness of breath, choking, sighing, and an empty feeling in the abdomen; a feeling of general weakness, and an intense subjective distress described as tension or mental pain. These experiences are usually accompanied by preoccupation with images of the deceased, guilt, hostile reactions, and the loss of patterns of conduct. He noted the tendency to "avoid the syndrome at any cost, to refuse visits lest they should precipitate the reaction, and to keep deliberately from the thought of all references to the deceased."[19]

Lindemann discussed resolution of bereavement, employing Freud's term "the work of mourning." He depicted the bereaved person struggling to deal with physiological symptoms (sighing respiration, lack of strength), preoccupation with images of the deceased, feelings of guilt, often a disconcerting loss of warmth in relationship with people, and feelings of hostility toward others that were inexplicable and disturbing to the bereaved. He observed that the duration of a grief reaction seems to depend upon how effectively a person does the *grief work*—namely, "emancipation from the bondage to the deceased, readjustment to the environment in which the deceased is missing, and the formation of new relationships. One of the big obstacles to this work seems to be the fact that many patients try to avoid the intense distress connected with the grief experience and to avoid the expression of emotion necessary for it."[20]

Lindemann concluded that working through mourning entails accepting the reality that the only contact with the loved one is through memory. When this occurs, there is often a rapid relief of tension in the bereaved, and subsequent counseling sessions are animated conversations in which the deceased is idealized, and misgivings about the future adjustment are worked through.[21]

On the other hand, morbid grief reactions usually were characterized by delayed reaction to the loss or by distorted reactions—for example, overactivity without a sense of loss, acquisition of symptoms of the last illness of the deceased, a recognized medical disease, alterations (sometimes lasting) in relationships with friends or family, exaggerated hostility, or activities which might be detrimental to the bereaved person's social or economic existence; or agitated depression. Lindemann also included in his research the concept of "anticipatory grief"—for example, that of a family facing the departure of a member into the armed forces. Among the most valuable of his contributions were his suggestions for the management of both normal and morbid grief.

Discussion of the grief process through the 1960s remained largely within the orbit of psychoanalytic theory. In England, psychiatrist Colin Murray Parkes concluded that "if the psychoanalytic theory of depression is correct, then all depressive illnesses are a species of mourning and it is to be expected that such illnesses will be particularly common following bereavement."[22] His first research project investigated the incidence of recent bereavement in the preillness histories of patients. Among 3,245 patients admitted to a psychiatric unit between 1949–1951, three percent were presented within six months of the death of a parent, spouse, sibling, or child. Further, the number of patients whose illness followed the loss of a spouse was six times greater than expected, suggesting that bereavement contributed to the development of the illness. He noted that there was a preponderance of women over forty, and that the incidence of affective disorders, particularly of reactive and neurotic depressions, was significantly greater among bereaved than among non-bereaved patients.

In 1972, Parkes wrote that doctors often "treat" grief. He suggested:

> There are indications that many people go to their doctor for help after a bereavement, and a large proportion of their complaints, as I shall show, are expressions of grief. . . . Illnesses are characterized by the discomfort and the disturbance of function that they produce. Grief may not produce physical pain but it is very unpleasant and it usually disturbs function. *Thus a newly bereaved person is often treated by society in much the same way as a sick person* [emphasis added].[23]

He added that he knew of only one functional psychiatric disorder whose cause is known, whose features are distinctive, and whose course is usually predictable—that is, grief, the reaction to loss.[24]

Until the work of Lindemann, attention had been directed toward the role of grief in the study of psychopathology. Two significant trends emerged: First, the symptomatology of "normal grief" became the subject of research; second, researchers began to differentiate grief due to bereavement from other sources of grief. Now Parkes took up the latter issue. He reiterated an aspect of grief noted earlier by Shakespeare and Samuel Johnson—that grief may be evoked by any perceived loss or change, of which bereavement is merely the most easily recognized instance. He declared that loss and deprivation are so inseparably bound together that it is impossible to study one apart from the other, though he claimed that bereavement is a different order of grief:

> There is one thing that justifies us in treating bereavement as a unitary stress and paying less attention to secondary losses, deprivation, role change, and stigma, namely, the observation that grief is so powerful a reaction that, for a time, it overshadows all other sources of difficulty. "For my particular grief," says Brabantio, "Is of so floodgate and o'erbearing nature, That it engluts and swallows other sorrows, And it is still itself." [*Othello* I.ii][25]

Nevertheless, attention must be given to the comprehensive and universal impact of (general) grief. People face many changes in their lives: "Arriving, departing, growing, declining, achieving, failing—every change involves a loss and a gain. The old environment must be given up, the new accepted. People come and go; one job is lost, another begun; territory and possessions are acquired or sold; new skills are learnt, old abandoned; expectations are fulfilled or hopes dashed.[26]

In all these situations individuals face the need to abandon one mode of life and accept another. Even when the change is "from worse to better" and acceptance relatively easy, grief may attach to the experience. But when it is a loss, a "mixed blessing," most will do their best to resist change. "Resistance to change, the reluctance to give up possessions, people, status, expectations—this, I believe, is the basis of grief."[27]

This concept was developed by Peter Marris, a British sociologist, who provided a carefully documented argument for this expanded notion of grief. He noted that, in his perception, the concept of grieving could be applied to many situations of change which we would not ordinarily think of as grief. That is, he continued, "Whenever people suffered loss—even though they might also desire change— their reactions expressed an internal conflict, whose nature was fundamentally similar to the working out of grief."[28] He uses the term *grieving* to refer to the psychological process of adjustment to loss: "Grieving reactions are evoked when adaptive abilities are threatened. In this sense grieving is a more inclusive concept than the obvious, extreme emotional distress which the bereaved may express. The more or less conventional, institutionalized expressions of grief I have called 'mourning.' "[29]

Like other researchers, Marris argued that resistance to change is a fact of life, yet humans are the most adaptable of all living creatures. He identified reluctance to change as a "conservative impulse," as necessary for survival as adaptability. The assimilation of new experiences is achieved by placing them in the context of a familiar, reliable construction of reality, which, in turn, rests on the regularity of events as well as the continuity of their meaning.[30] In this sense we are all profoundly conservative, and feel immediately threatened if our basic assumptions and emotional attachments are threatened. Marris's argument rests upon three propositions:

1. The construction of meaningful perceptions is cumulative, so that the more fundamental the revisions that have to be made, the more of the structure must be dismantled and the more disruptive revision becomes.
2. The purposive context of meaning seems less open to revision than the ordering of events according to the regularities of experience—that is, we cannot command our feelings or reverse feelings, or reverse the experiences through which our emotional needs have acquired a habit of attachment.
3. Meanings are learned in the context of specific relationships and circumstances, and we may not readily see how to translate them to an apparently different context.[31]

Marris concludes that the irretrievable loss of the familiar must be followed by a reinterpretation of what we have learned about our purposes and attachments that is radical enough to trace out the thread again: "To do this, the loss must first be accepted as something we have to understand. . . . The conservative impulse will make us seek to deny the loss. But when this fails, it will also lead us to repair the thread, trying past, present and future together again with rewoven strands of meaning."[32]

Worden, together with Glenn W. Davidson, represents a new thrust in the area of grief recognition and response. Worden provides one of the most comprehensive aids to professionals who counsel bereaved people. His work began in 1968 with an investigation of terminal illness and suicide, and was enlarged to include others areas within the general scope of life-threatening illness and life-threatening behavior.[33] Pastors will be well repaid by careful study of his presentation of grief therapy.

Davidson's study of dying and death began in 1960 with graduate research related to images of death in America.[34] As with other researchers, Davidson expands the scope of the grief process to include reaction to loss and change: "We are born with the *ability* to adapt to change, but we all must *learn* how to cope with loss." In order to cope with loss, he suggests, "We need to learn to respect the natural psychological process that helps us recover emotionally from the shock of loss and from the suffering of deprivation. Our natural way is to mourn, to grieve."[35] Second, mourning is a developmental and lifelong process. As with Worden's volume, this is a book with which pastors should be familiar, and from which laypeople will benefit.

The Response of Pastoral Theologians

By the mid-1950s, ministry to bereaved members of congregations had attracted the attention of pastoral theologians. Edgar N. Jackson was one of the first to explore the significance for pastoral care to people in grief of new insights from the social sciences.[36] Jackson stated that most grief situations are normal; the great majority of people meet life's crises with enough strength and momentum to work through them, often surprising themselves with their newly discovered capacities. This progress is enhanced by clergy-initiated pastoral care: "The minister, as the person designated by society to deal with the needs of the bereaved, should be aware of the importance of his function. . . . He has a chance to engage the personalities of the grief-stricken in the constructive work of mourning, and he is guilty of professional negligence if he fails to do wisely and well what he is called upon to do."[37]

Jackson warned that, often from lack of awareness of the emotions

and needs of the bereaved, clergy "say and do things that make the
work of mourning more difficult and delay the normal processes of
withdrawing the ego investment and placing the emotional capital
elsewhere."[38] Jackson pointed to the pioneering work of Lindemann,
who had referred to the leading role that religious agencies had played
in dealing with the bereaved. Jackson proposed three roles for clergy,
drawing on suggestions made by Lindemann:

1. Clergy should maintain contact with grieving members,
   providing the sustained communication with a trusted individual
   which relieves emotional stress and guarantees a measure of
   emotional security. Clergy should be able to communicate full
   information concerning physical matters to the bereaved, so that
   the reality relationship will be maintained and confidence in the
   counselor made secure.
2. Clergy should be able to deliver messages that are important to
   the bereaved so they can be interpreted and related to other
   events that are happening. The pastor should help grieving
   members to manage those tasks and functions which are within
   their power to perform, and relieve the stress where it appears to
   be too taxing.
3. When indicated, the pastor should help grieving people to face the
   reality of their situations and think through the deeper meanings of
   their new responsibilities, new relationships, and problems of
   adjustment. The pastor "should be the backboard against which
   the mourner can work out his new thoughts and feelings."[39]

Jackson also drew attention to Lindemann's nine proposed areas of
concern for caregivers who counsel people in grief. Clergy must be
ready to assist bereaved members to accept the pain of their grief;
review relationships with deceased loved ones; explore their feelings
and how they have changed; interpret new feelings they are
experiencing and relieve their fear that they are losing their minds;
process changed feelings and assess what they are able to accomplish
toward working through them; acknowledge and understand hostility,
if it is present; decide how they should think and feel about the
deceased; verbalize and understand feelings of guilt; and explore new
modes of living and relations with new people.[40]

Jackson warned his readers that bereaved members may assume a
relationship of dependency upon caregivers which may be temporary,
but sometimes may be prolonged. Pastors must be able to recognize

when it is a useful and healthy dependency, and when it ceases to be useful. They must also beware of premature severing of dependency, due, for example, to the need to turn their attention to other members in need of pastoral support. The pastor's alternative to withdrawal of clergy support is the development of group relationships—grief-support groups—in which grief may be socialized: "The normal life of the [congregation] includes a variety of group activities which may well serve the needs of the person who is emerging from a period of mourning." Finally, it is the pastor's function to sustain bereaved members, remaining alert to those whose disturbance calls for the treatment of a specialist. "Lindemann makes this explicit in these words: 'Ministers will have to be on the look-out for the more ominous pictures, referring these to the psychiatrist while assisting the more normal reactions themselves.' "[41]

Granger Westberg was also one of the early authors from the field of pastoral care to address the subject of grief ministry. In 1961, he published *Minister and Doctor Meet*[42] in which he called for a closer working relationship between clergy and physicians. Based on a chapter in that book, *Good Grief* was published in 1962 and is now in its thirtieth printing.[43]

Westberg differentiates between "little griefs" and "large griefs." Among the former, he includes disappointments, change of employment, moving, one's child leaving home, failure to achieve an anticipated promotion, and breach in a relationship. Grief, which is "as natural as breathing," is addressed in reference to ten "stages": the state of shock, expression of emotion, feelings of depression and loneliness, physical symptoms of distress, feelings of panic, a sense of guilt, feelings of anger and resentment, resistance to getting back into life again, the emergence of hope, and the struggle to affirm reality.

Westberg suggests that people respond to grief in different ways and that caregivers should not attempt to force others to meet their expectations about the form they think another's bereavement should take:

> The ten stages of grief must be understood to be the *normal* process through which most people must go as they face up to their loss. In other words, we [are] talking about the road the majority of humans must travel in order to get back into the mainstream of life. . . . Remember that every person does not necessarily go through all these stages, nor does a person necessarily go through them in this order. Moreover, it is impossible to differentiate clearly between each of these stages, for a person never moves neatly from one to the other.[44]

A review of the literature from both the social sciences and theology indicates that since the 1960s there has been an intense, growing effort to understand grief—its etiology, psychological structure, impact on people's lives, and the meanings assigned by grieving people to their experiences. Within the sphere of *pastoral* theology efforts have been made to interpret for clergy what has been learned from the social sciences and to set these perceptions and meanings within relevant theological contexts. *The Journal of Pastoral Care* and *Pastoral Psychology* regularly publish articles on grief and grief ministry. The latter, for instance, published special grief issues beginning in the late 1950s.[45]

An important article was published by *The Journal of Pastoral Care* in 1979, in which R. Scott Sullender reviewed three of the most widely used theoretical models.[46] He noted that the universality of grief experiences might lead one to assume that the task of defining grief would be easy. On the contrary, he writes, grief is a process that is always changing and becoming. Second, the nature and extent of grief varies with the type of loss involved; the death of a loved one differs from the loss of a valued object. Third, grief reactions vary widely from one individual to another, because of the uniqueness of each human being. Fourth, grief reactions vary with particular cultures, and even within cultures, subcultures, and family systems. He identifies the three models as follows.

1. *Grief as Reaction to Loss.* He identifies Parkes with this concept, which emphasizes that life "is filled with an infinite variety of losses, some major, many more gradual and routine, but each one being potentially an occasion for grief." Any life change can be a loss event, and therefore potentially an occasion for grief.

2. *Grief as Separation Anxiety.* Sullender cites David Switzer,[47] who extended the work of Harry Stack Sullivan. Switzer notes that acute grief is remarkably similar to a classic anxiety attack, as documented by psychoanalytic writers, complete with defense mechanisms. This leads him to the conclusion that grief is a form of anxiety—namely, "separation anxiety," for which talking as a way of symbolically and conceptually "staying close" to the lost love object is still the best remedy.

3. *Grief as a Function of Attachment Instincts.* This view, beginning with Freud, was developed by John Bowlby and Parkes, as well as by William Rogers, an early writer in the pastoral care movement, who suggest that grief exists because the griever valued

and gave meaning to that which is now lost—that is, grief is a function of attachment. On this basis, we may have a clue to the answer to a frequently asked question: "How should one interpret the response of a person who does not seem to grieve with the intensity one would have expected?" Part of the answer, of course, is that the mourner may be masking a deeply felt grief because of his or her inability to mourn publicly or the need to do so in private; or it may be that lack of public grief reflects a similar lack of intensity of bonding with the deceased. One can imagine other possible explanations.

Sullender notes that Bowlby understands separation anxiety, grief, and mourning as a continuing process. Grief begins as separation anxiety and protest, with the assumption that absence is temporary. After a prolonged absence or when that absence is deemed permanent from the start, the slow, painful process of emotional detachment is begun. "Only when grief does its work, and successfully frees the griever's emotional energy from the lost object, can that person reinvest him/herself in new objects of attachment. Grief in this sense is necessary for health, both the health of the individual and of the social unit."[48]

Sullender notes the interdependence of the three conceptual models, but concludes that each offers a unique perspective into the nature of grief. He depicts grief as the emotional reaction that begins when a person perceives that he or she has *lost* (or been separated from) something (or someone) of emotional *attachment*. He regards *separation anxiety* as the irreducible element in grief, particularly in its early stages: "Grief's purpose is to emotionally detach people from that which is now lost, thus enabling them to reinvest themselves in new attachments. Grief is therefore necessary, and even essential, for good psychological health."[49]

Gaps in Congregations' Grief Ministries

This brief review of sources indicates both their scope and the common thread that runs through much of the literature and focuses on the concept of grief as "work." Since the 1960s, there has been a spate of publications on the subject of grief viewed from the perspective of pastoral theology and pastoral care, mirroring a comparable flood tide from the social sciences.[50] As a result, most clergy seem to be familiar with commonly held notions of "the grief process," and many have attended seminars with Elisabeth Kubler-Ross. Yet many appear to have failed to translate their understanding of this process into effective congregational care of bereaved families. Sampling indicates that, apart from support provided to bereaved members by church-school classes and other organized congregational groups, consistent, intentional grief ministry is largely lacking in American congregations.

The conversations and discussions that led to this conclusion began in June 1989, when Service Corporation International (SCI) Inc. instituted a nationwide lecture program for clergy and other community caregivers. Service Corporation is a public company listed on the New York Stock Exchange and is the largest owner and operator of funeral homes in North America. In 1989, the company launched a community-service program based on the production of a half-hour videotape titled "Working Through Your Grief." I prepared the text on which the video was based, and, with other seminar lecturers, introduced the videotape through community-grief seminars sponsored by the company's participating funeral homes. The video provides a general introduction to the types of emotional impact the death of a loved one may have on a bereaved person or family, and the means bereaved people may use to work through their grief. Clergy and other community caregivers attending the seminars viewed the videotape and were advised that the tape is provided without cost—not only to client families of the respective SCI funeral homes but to any family in their communities. Clergy, hospice staffs, and grief-support agencies are invited to use the video in their ministries to bereaved individuals and families, and in their grief education programs.[51]

In the course of seminar presentations during the period from September 1989 through June 1990, I met more than 2,000 clergy and 4,000 laypeople in 70 cities. Groups ranged in size from 30 to 300 and included representatives of Jewish, Catholic, mainline Protestant, and a broad range of independent congregational clergy. The two most common elements shared by the clergy groups were their recognition of the work of Elisabeth Kubler-Ross as the source of their awareness of "the grief process," and the failure of their congregations to translate their understanding of this process into effective care of bereaved families. This will be addressed in a subsequent chapter. Chapter 2 examines the contribution of Kubler-Ross as a first step toward substituting the notion of completing the tasks of mourning for the more familiar "stages" of grief.

CHAPTER 2

Working
Through Grief

Who alone suffers suffers most i' the mind.
KING LEAR III.vi.111

The Contribution of Elisabeth Kubler-Ross[1]

The majority of clergy whom I met in the period from September 1989 through June 1990 appeared unfamiliar with the extensive literature on dying, death, and bereavement published since 1950. About 50 percent were familiar with Westberg's *Good Grief*, which remains one of the best sources to place in the hands of bereaved families, though it is limited by its dependence on the now outworn notion of "stages" of grief. In contrast to these perceptions, almost all clergy were familiar with Kubler-Ross's first book, *On Death and Dying*, and most possessed and had read the volume.[2]

Dying, death, and bereavement are life experiences common to every individual. They have been part of human life for a long time! It seems all the more inexplicable, therefore, that attempts to analyze and understand their meaning have been so recent. An examination of bibliographies on these topics reveals that of the approximately 10,000 entries, the vast majority are dated since 1970! The publication of *On Death and Dying* coincided with a vast expansion of the themes and materials first identified by Freud, Lindemann, Parkes, Jackson, and other early writers. By the early 1970s, the new "movement" had taken two directions: first, intensive research into the psychodynamics of grief; and second, public awareness of the subject, manifested, for example, in large audiences attending Kubler-Ross's public lectures.

Kubler-Ross recounts that, in 1965, she assisted four seminary students in a research project on crises in human life. They elected to confine their investigation to the crisis of dying. As resistance from physicians was overcome and interviews with dying patients progressed, patterned responses began to emerge. It appears that these have been internalized simplistically by most readers in the format: denial, anger, bargaining, depression, and acceptance, the so-called Five Stages. Worse, they seem to be remembered as "The Five Stages of *Grief*." In its most rudimentary form, people have selectively remembered the format as a mechanical, or linear, response to grief, or, in the case of the dying person, anticipatory grief, as seen in Figure 1:

Denial ⟶ Anger ⟶ Bargaining ⟶ Depression ⟶ Acceptance

That is, the dying person can be expected to traverse the five "stages," moving discernibly from one to the next and emerging successfully at "acceptance."

Such an interpretation of the theme of *On Death and Dying* is a caricature that does not do justice to the author's presentation. First, Kubler-Ross referred to these responses in dying patients as "The Five Stages of *Dying*." Second, at almost every point, Kubler-Ross qualified her findings. For example, she states that *denial* is usually a temporary defense soon replaced by partial acceptance; most patients do not use denial extensively. Kubler-Ross also found that patients are selective in choosing with whom, among family members, friends, and hospital staff, they will discuss matters of their illness or impending death, while evading those issues with people who cannot tolerate the thought of their death.

Similar qualifications are made with respect to the remaining "stages." Kubler-Ross illustrates each term with appropriate cases. They indicate the responses people manifest when they are faced with crises—that is, coping devices to deal with difficult situations that will last for different periods of time and replace each other, or at times exist, side by side.

The publication of *On Death and Dying* conincided with a widespread eagerness to move discussions of dying, death, and grieving into the public domain. Her reporting of her openness with dying patients contributed to greater public openness to discussion of this fundamental aspect of human life. Yet she has decried attempts to idealize her contribution. When a PBS television interviewer elaborated eloquently on her work some years ago, she replied: "I am a doctor, but I never healed anyone. I certainly never found a cure for a disease. All I ever did was sit and listen to people, and *hear* them." But because her original contribution has too often been perceived and presented by others in an oversimplified manner, many people have been left with a simplistic concept of grief, which now can be corrected.

The first problem arises from the mistranslation of the five stages of dying as "The Five Stages of *Grief.*" Kubler-Ross was specific that her data and perceptions were derived from conversations with patients who faced impending death, and it was the pattern of their responses she was documenting. It is misleading to transfer these categories to the generic term *grief*, which, as previous researchers in the social sciences have demonstrated, includes not only mourning, the process that characterizes bereavement, but refers to a wide range of perceived losses and changes.

More important, the term *stages* is misleading. Kubler-Ross used the term loosely, as suggestive of the responses of most dying people most of the time. However, it tends to assume a concrete, arbitrary, and mechanical or linear nature and progression, as represented by the medical intern who objected to the attending physician: "But Mrs. Johnson can't die yet. She hasn't gone through the bargaining stage!" When, as caregivers, we attempt to discern in which "stage" of grief a person should be placed—when we are more concerned with our own psychologizing—we are apt to miss the *person* and his or her deepest anxieties and needs. That treats people as objects and is too high a risk to take.

Finally, in any case, there are not *five* stages. Lindemann suggested *nine* common, or normative, grief responses. Robert White and Leroy Gathman identify *three* basic stages,[3] while Westberg indicates there are *ten!*[4] Each is an attempt to create images, or draw pictures, to help us understand the responses which most people appear to experience as they mourn loved ones who have died. But if it is inadvisable to refer to them as "stages, how are they to be categorized?

The alternative already existed in the grief literature. First, Sigmund Freud, followed by almost every succeeding observer, recognized that resolving grief is hard work. It is to this fundamental aspect of grief that we must give our attention.

The *Work* of Mourning

Caregivers will gain a clearer understanding of how grief may best be resolved and bereaved people helped more effectively to *work* through grief if attention is focused on the *tasks of mourning* that must be addressed by the grieving person.

1. *Accepting the Reality of the Loss*

Freud first drew attention to the task of accepting the reality of the loss: "Reality passes its verdict—that the object no longer exists . . . and the ego . . . is persuaded . . . to sever its attachment to the non-existent object."[5] Klein concluded that this testing of reality is one of the essential tasks of mourning. Lindemann concurred, stating that the duration of a grief reaction seems to depend upon the success with which a person does the *grief work*. He identified three tasks which must be faced: emancipation from the bondage to the deceased, readjustment to the changed environment, and the formation of new relationships.[6] Later researchers have expanded Lindemann's notion of grief work, as follows:

a. *Emancipation from Bondage to the Deceased*

William Worden is the most recent author to emphasize the importance of this task. Noting that when someone dies there is always a sense that it has not happened (even if the death has been expected), "the first task of grieving is to come full face with the reality that the person is dead, that the person is gone and will not return."[7] Accepting that reunion is not possible, "at least in this life," Worden suggests that the searching behavior noted by Parkes and Bowlby directly relates to the accomplishment of this task. He warns that denying the fact of the loss can vary in degree from a slight distortion to a full-blown delusion.

From accounts of survivors, grief reactions on the one hand may be manifested in a widow daily setting her deceased husband's place at the table, placing his slippers at the beside nightly, or conducting "conversations" with the deceased. It may, however, extend to speaking of a deceased child in the present tense and maintaining that the child is "away" but will return at a time to be arranged. Decisions to keep a deceased child's room untouched for months or even years, including leaving discarded books and toys on the floor where they were dropped, may represent an effort to maintain the figment that the child needs to be able to recognize the room upon his or her "return."

Other illustrations of efforts to avoid doing the hard work of accepting the reality of death are provided by Worden,[8] Marris,[9] and Parkes.[10] Marris quotes Geoffrey Gorer's citation of a widower's response to his wife's death: "I was upstairs after the wife died and I was watching television for the first time after she died; and all of a sudden I could see my wife as plain as anything, sitting in one of these chairs. I flew downstairs and never went in that room again."[11]

b. Accepting the Pain and Readjusting to the Environment

The choice to meet the pain fullface and begin to adjust to the absence of the loved one is a difficult and painful task. It marks the final abandonment of the dream somehow to recapture the deceased through use of devices like those described above, and to turn one's face toward the future, knowing one will not enjoy the physical company and support of the deceased. For example, it means, for some widows, undertaking tasks like balancing a checkbook, making business decisions without the consultation of a spouse, or remembering that children will not graduate with their peers or grow up so that parent and child may relate as adults, friends, and confidants. Addressing this task means that the bereaved person has chosen to admit the pain into conscious, day-to-day decision-making and face other daily responsibilities, many of which stir up memories of the deceased.

Sally, an eighty-year-old widow, is one of the participants in a grief-support group dramatized in the videotape "Working Through Your Grief." She describes how, a few days after her husband's death, she was working in the garden and, fearful of ceasing her chores and entering the empty house, continued until darkness forced her to stop: "I started to work, and it got late. I just kept on working, but I wasn't going to quit and go inside. I kept telling myself that I would wait for Paul to call me in. . . . Finally, it got so late that I wasn't sure whether I was pulling up weeds or my flowers. It was at that point, kneeling in the flowerbed, I sort of came to and realized that he wouldn't be calling me any more."[12]

In a similar vein, June, a junior-high teacher, described to me how she returned to the staff room following a class session. The room was empty, and as she began to grade student papers, she recalled her daughter's death three months earlier. Reflecting that Jeannie would not graduate with the class she was teaching, she pictured what it would have been like to have her daughter go shopping with her as an adult, knowing that would not happen now. Tears gathered in her eyes. Another staff member entered the room, and her response only deepened June's feeling of loss. Seeing the tears on June's cheeks, the other teacher blurted out, "Oh, for goodness' sake, June, it's been three months!"

2. Working Through Painful Feelings

Our feelings are a very important part of our daily lives; we are constantly experiencing feelings and responding to them. We may not always be able to put labels on them—we may be angry, for example, and act out our anger or retreat from dealing with it—without consciously analyzing either our feelings or our responses. Some feelings may cause great discomfort and block our capacity to carry on customary daily activities. That applies particularly to responses to the feelings often generated by bereavement.

Feelings of shock, numbness, and disbelief are characteristic of the early period of bereavement, often accompanied by feelings of intense anxiety, evoked by the mourner's fear of "going crazy." Westberg notes: "When a person begins worrying about losing his mind, he often panics. He becomes almost paralyzed with fear. It is often fear of the unknown, or fear of something he does not understand, that throws him into a panic."[13] Worden uses more clinical terminology, referring to hallucinations, both visual and auditory, which he includes in his list of "normal" behaviors in bereaved people, because of the frequency with which they are experienced: "They are usually transient . . . often occurring within a few weeks following the loss, and generally do not portend a more difficult or complicated mourning experience."[14]

Anger is one feeling we may need to work through. But there is a host of other feelings that often crowd the days and nights of the grief-stricken: sadness, which may be expressed by a mild disappointment, or a more intense experience that may deepen into depression; loneliness, isolation, or alienation; helplessness, and sometimes, panic; shame, remorse, and guilt; fear, anxiety, or despair; relief and emancipation. These feelings are appropriate to the sense of loss suffered in bereavement, but because we differ individually from one another, we experience them with differing intensities and durations, and our reactions to them will reflect the types of responses we have developed individually over our respective lifetimes. Many of us spend little time "processing" our feelings. We usually experience and react to them, put them aside, and go on with our daily lives, yet they may preoccupy much of our time at various levels of conscious or unconscious activity.

a. Resolving Anger

Bereaved people are not necessarily angry. Many mourners are not faced with this task, and one of the problems arising from the caricature of the Kubler-Ross taxonomy has been the emergence of the notion that anger is endemic to grief. For some individuals, it may be. I was invited to attend a meeting of a Compassionate Friends chapter and arrived to find a group of eighty parents seated in a circle.[15] They all introduced themselves by name, adding the name of the child who had died, and the cause of death. A fifty-five-year-old man, present for the first time, stood and, for fifteen minutes, raged at his son's untimely death from leukemia. He related that his son had taken every honor in pathology courses during medical school, had served a brilliant residency, again receiving many honors, had been acclaimed as a pathology fellow, and finally had been appointed to the faculty of his medical school. Now, we were told, death had robbed the community of one of its most brilliant sons. The father raged at God, life's injustices, and the supreme waste of one who would have made an extraordinary contribution to medicine had he only lived. At the close of the meeting, I learned that his son had died five years earlier and wondered how he had lived with a rage so intense, and how it had shaped his relationships with his family, neighbors, and associates where he worked.

Twelve months later, I again attended a meeting of the group. The same man was present, and, in his turn, introduced himself by stating his name, his son's name, and how he had died. His participation in the Compassionate Friends chapter had provided him with a place in which it was acceptable and "safe" to voice his anger and resolve it sufficiently that his life now was not so driven by unremitting rage. It is not that he will never again be stirred to anger at the loss of his gifted son, but that the flood of his anger had ebbed, and the river is back within its banks.

A funeral director shared with me the story of a nine-year-old boy whose father had died. During the family visitation at the funeral home prior to the funeral, a well-meaning adult saw the boy sitting alone by the casket and offered his comfort: "You must not cry, Frank. God needs your dad more than you do." Unaware of the remark, Frank's mother became alarmed as the weeks passed and Frank refused to accompany her to Sunday school or worship, growing morose and difficult to manage both at home and in school. His teachers phoned her to arrange a conference to address the problem of inappropriate outbursts during class.

Disturbed, she called the funeral director, described these events, and expressed her sense of helplessness. Through his contacts with the Big Brother program, a volunteer was assigned to Frank. Frank's "big brother" gradually won his confidence. During a Saturday outing, he shared what had been said to him the night before his father's funeral. He shouted angrily: "I hate God! I hate God!" Over the next few weeks, guided by their pastor, the "brother" accepted Frank's anger and provided a setting in which to explore a more wholesome image of God as one who shared his hurt rather than caused it. Who can say what measure of harm would have endured, had not the anger and its source been addressed and resolved?

The task of working through anger evoked by the death of a loved one is complicated by a common misperception that anger is a sin. I walked into a seminary classroom to begin a lecture, and finding that the previous teacher had listed the "seven deadly sins" on the board, was prompted to erase "anger" and replace "seven" by "six." I suspect that one of our earliest impressions is that of the sinful nature of anger. Yet God is often presented as angry with Israel, Moses, and on occasion, with the prophets. Jesus' anger was expressed not only toward the religious authorities but toward his disciples. It is obviously possible to be angry but not sin. Yet the impression is emphasized throughout childhood: Do not be angry! As a child, I often wondered why it was acceptable for parents or teachers to be angry with me, but never permissible for me to express anger to adults. But anger is no more a sin than is money, sex, or power. Of course, each can be used in destructive, sinful ways, but that is saying something entirely different.

The task of mourning is more painful when anger, if perceived as sinful, is evoked by the sense of loss. When death is shrouded in tragedy and experienced as unfair or unjust, the grieving person may often feel robbed. Indeed, the verb "to be bereaved" stems from the Old German root *berauben*, passing into old English as the verb *"to be reaved"*—that is, "robbed." In this context, especially if directed toward God, feelings of anger can lead to guilt which may further intensify and prolong grief.

The authority vested in the clergy office may be a channel through which pastors may minister to people whose grief is prolonged because they are unable to resolve such anger or its related guilt.

Grief similarly may be prolonged when anger is felt toward the deceased. Eda LeShan writes to children mourning the death of a parent. She suggests they may find themselves asking, "How could Daddy leave me if he really loved me?" or "Didn't Mommy care what happens to me?" She continues: "You may feel that you have been deserted and that makes you very, very angry—even though you know perfectly well that your parent could not help getting sick or being in an accident. Feelings sometimes have little or nothing to do with the facts. But feeling angry usually makes us feel guilty."[16] Such feelings are painful but must be worked through if the tasks of mourning are to be completed sufficiently so that the grieving person can go on with life.

b. Laying Aside the Regrets

Kubler-Ross noted from her conversations with dying patients that many resorted to what she termed "bargaining" in an effort to buy time, presumably from God. I was called to the hospital emergency center late one Saturday afternoon by the charge nurse, who urged me to be there before the arrival of the ambulance they were expecting. It was bringing Timmy, a five-year-old boy who had been run over by a car driven by his father—one of those domestic accidents that can happen so unexpectedly. Timmy's mother had asked her husband a number of times to interrupt his Saturday chores to complete the weekend shopping.

"And don't forget to take Timmy," she had added. "I promised him that he could go with you to the store." When he was able to set his work aside, he looked for his son but was unable to find him. Impatiently, he started the car and reversed down the drive. In the meantime, Timmy had returned from playing with his friends in the street and, on entering his front yard, heard the car engine start. He ran across the lawn into the driveway—and into the path of the car.

The ambulance arrived at the emergency center, and Timmy was rushed into the trauma room. I spend most of the next two hours with Timmy's parents. They sat in silence, numbed with shock, their eyes meeting occasionally with unspoken expressions of accusation or guilt. Suddenly the silence was broken by a cry from Timmy's dad: "Oh, God, let Timmy live! I'll take him to Sunday school every Sunday!"

While one may be uncomfortable with the implicit theology, the cry of pain is certainly real and understandable. Timmy's dad will probably carry his guilt throughout his life, and statistically, there is a high probability the marriage will dissolve.

Regrets and remorse, however, may be evoked by far less traumatic events or perceptions, or real or imagined omissions. If not addressed, such regrets may verge into remorse and last a lifetime. In the event that remorse and guilt are responses to a grief intensified by self-blame due to actions taken or not taken, lives and family relationships may be critically impaired. A woman in a small Midwest city tearfully shared her story with me:

> When I was seven years old, scarlet fever went through our school, and I spent two weeks in bed. About two weeks after I went back to school, my father became very ill and died. A few days later, I overheard two of my aunts discussing my father's sudden illness: "However could he have contracted scarlet fever?" asked one aunt. "Didn't you know? Jenny brought it back from her school." That was fifty years ago, and you are the first person I have told. For fifty years, I thought I killed my father.

If death has already occurred, there clearly is little point in attempting to "bargain back" a life. Our subsequent attempts to deal with bereavement with an anguish-filled "If only . . ." may, in fact, be a belated expression of bargaining. Too late to alter events, and to that extent pointless, we nevertheless find ourselves saying, "If only I had been there . . ." or "If only he had been more careful. . . ." Our "if onlys" demonstrate how we may cling to the possibility that we could have averted death. Such images may be another means of evading the moving on through the painful task of mourning. As with other devices we use to put off this task, it is understandable, and simply illustrates the intensity of the pain we choose either to confront and work through, or to evade, even though that is often to our cost.

c. Struggling Through the Sadness

The symptoms described by bereaved people often are those of depression: marked sighing respirations, a feeling of emotional distance from others, and sensations of somatic distress—for example, tightness in the throat, an empty feeling in the stomach, weakness, and a feeling of tension or mental pain. The problem is that the term *depression* encompasses a range of meanings, varying from lay usages to clinical or pathological states. A person in acute grief who becomes deeply depressed may be referred for psychotherapy. Lindemann,[17] Parkes,[18] and Marris[19] describe the typical symptoms pertaining to depression used in its lay sense. The person in "uncomplicated" grief characterized by appropriate levels of sadness may be supported by family, friends, or pastors, and require little in the way of counseling. Worden states: "Sadness is the most common feeling found in the bereaved and really needs little comment. This feeling is not necessarily manifested by crying behavior, but it often is."[20] We do know that in many western cultures, crying as an expression of sadness is permitted of women but not of men, who are expected not to "fall apart," to "keep a stiff upper lip." Boys are reminded that "men do not cry."

People in most western societies often given the appearance of being uncomfortable with displays of sadness. Many are so ill at ease that they choose not to attend funerals, for example, excusing their absence by explaining that they "would not know what to say." Intimate and even casual contacts with bereaved families may be ended quickly—many bereaved people report that significant support from their congregations ended as early as seven days after the funeral. Acquaintances may cross the street to avoid meeting a recently bereaved neighbor. If these reported perceptions accurately represent how people generally respond to the needs of bereaved families, the case is already made for education programs, through which people may learn more effective ways to support people in mourning.

Caregivers must first come to terms with their own pain evoked by the pain in the lives of others. Most people feel discomfort when in pain, and since we prefer not to experience pain, we try to avoid it. One way to do so is not to be with other people when they are distressed. The tragedy is that such avoidance of people in mourning leaves them isolated in their grief, an experience that may leave them confused and often embittered. They feel that others have already forgotten them and their deceased loved ones. It is more likely that members of congregations are simply protecting themselves from the pain of the mourner's grief, but that avoidance is perceived as a lack of compassion. The SCI videotape, *Working Through Your Grief,* portrays a grieving father who talks of his growing anger since the recent death of his twenty-three-year-old son, Steve. His support group helps him focus his anger: "It's my neighbors. . . . They never even mention Steve's name! It's as if he never existed. I don't know why they seem embarrassed to talk about him. They used to think the world of him. Now it makes me wonder if they've forgotten all about him already."[21]

Grief researchers appear to have committed little research time to *sadness.* This is perhaps understandable—human sadness is less susceptible to analysis, perhaps, than other aspects of grief and is a theme that may be addressed more appropriately by novelists and poets. Their images suggest that, apart from psychosis (for example, Shakespeare's King Lear or Ophelia), the only way out of grief is through the travail of sorrow. This "painful toil" is expressed vividly by Alice Hoffman in *At Risk,* in which she tells the story of Polly and Ivan, the parents of Amanda, and their discovery that eleven-year-old Amanda has contracted AIDS.[22] Their pediatrician, Ed Reardon, called Ivan into his office to inform him of the diagnosis.

> [Ivan] has been crying since he left Ed Reardon's office, but now he begins to howl. . . . When the howling stops, Ivan sits motionless behind the steering wheel and he holds on to it. It crosses his mind that he should kill Ed Reardon. Ed is the one who diagnosed Amanda's appendicitis. There was unexpected bleeding during her surgery; Ivan remembers being told she needed a transfusion. That was when she was given the contaminated blood. For five years Ivan has been losing her without knowing it. Every time he has sent her to her room for being fresh, every time he missed a gymnastic meet, every hour he has spent looking at dead stars, he has been losing her. And now, on a Thursday morning, as blackbirds light on the bramble that grow alongside the road, he has lost her.[23]

And later:

> [Polly] can't turn to Ivan because if she did she would have to see how hurt he is. She can't look at Charlie [Amanda's brother], sitting out on the steps, waiting for a friend who will never appear. She can't listen to Madonna singing over and over again, "True love, oh baby," when she knows that her daughter will never stand in the dark on a summer night and, more aware of her own heart beating than of the mosquitoes circling the porch light, lean her head upward, toward her first kiss.[24]

Hoffman's book is a story about a family struggling to deal with the tragedy of AIDS. It is a story about a family's grief. The author traverses the full dimensions of her topic, portrayed graphically each member's roller-coaster plummeting through numbing paralysis, anguish, and rage. When Amanda suffers a relapse and Ed informs her parents that the end is near, Ivan turns to the wall and punches it: "Ivan is crying; he's not making a sound, but he's shaking all over. It's a terrible thing to see. . . . Ed goes over to Ivan and puts a hand on his shoulder, but Ivan jerks away. When Ivan finally does turn toward Ed his face is wet. 'This is my daughter!' Ivan says. 'She's eleven years old.' "[25]

When the sadness of people so bereft is unrelieved, either because, like Polly and Ivan, they are unable to share their pain, or because other potential caregivers are unable or unwilling to enter into that pain, grief may reach such a level of intensity that it may deepen into clinical depression. Thus, attention must be given to the relationship between grief and depression.

3. Struggling Back from Depression

Because the term *depression* is used in both professional and lay terms, confusion often arises when the user's intention is not specified. The relationship between grief and depression was first examined by Freud. The similarity of symptoms of "mild" depression and grief leads naturally to the link being drawn between them. Symptoms of sleep and appetite disturbance are common to both, and may be accompanied by intense sadness. Jackson suggests that bereaved people learn painfully to "let the past go" and turn their minds toward the future: "It may at first seem to be a bleak, impoverished future. But it is something you have to bring yourself to accept."[26] Yet it is just this having to "bring oneself to accept" the death of a loved one that is so painful, and which the bereaved person may find all sorts of ways to avoid facing.

The awareness that one is powerless to reverse the tide of events may be intensified by particular circumstances—for example, the age of the deceased, the unexpectedness of the death, or perceived injustices in the situation. Jackson notes that tragic or untimely death may lead to grief that is "made more poignant by our lack of understanding; it is made sharper by the fact that it was unexpected. It seems more cruel, because when death is sudden or untimely it always finds us in the midst of plans and hopes and dreams that must now be forever unfulfilled."[27]

The anguish that is appropriate to such grief may evoke responses that are difficult to differentiate from early indications of depression because, as indicated, the symptoms may overlap. Whereas one person may struggle back from intense sadness as the initial intensity of grief dissipates, another person may lapse further into self-pity, regrets, self-blame, or other immobilizing responses so that the border between sadness and depression is crossed. The difficulty, and even the impossibility, of "struggling back" from depression (in the "lay" sense) is known to most of us. We often trace this task when we are least able to marshal the strength or resources we need to recover our equilibrium. But it may be accomplished with the support of those family members or friends to whom we feel closest. The task of working through *clinical* depression usually requires more than just the support and encouragement of others. Herein lies the fundamental difference between grief and depression. The latter usually is compounded by a lack of self-esteem. Worden notes:

> In a grief reaction, there is not the loss of self-esteem commonly found in most clinical depressions. That is, the people who have lost someone do not regard themselves less because of such a loss or if they do, intend to be for only a brief time. And if the survivors of the deceased experience guilt, it is usually guilt associated with some specific aspect of the loss rather than a general, overall sense of culpability.[28]

He cites *Diagnostic and Statistical Manual III*, which states that a full depressive syndrome frequently is a normal reaction to such a loss, with feelings of depression and such associated symptoms as poor appetite, weight loss, and insomnia. However, morbid preoccupation with worthlessness, prolonged and marked functional impairment, and marked psychomotor retardation are uncommon.[29] Whereas, in responding to nonpathological grief, the bereaved person may feel depressed and recognized that it is within "normal" bounds, clinically depressed mourners are less likely to recognize all the implications of their state and may be unable to initiate measures to obtain relief. Pastors and concerned family members and friends should be alert to recognize when additional help is needed and make the appropriate referral for medical evaluation.

4. Deciding to Take Up One's Life Again

Prior to the death of the loved one, life has been going on in a more or less ordered way. Daily activities, responsibilities, and diversions have been met. When death intrudes, one enters the period of mourning and begins the tasks of accepting the reality of the loss: working through feelings like anger, sadness, anxiety; moving beyond regrets; and finding ways to fill the aching void created by loneliness and longing. The grieving person faces these tasks continually throughout the period of mourning. They are often so painful to face consciously that they may be set aside each time they surface. Deferring uncomfortable choices is a routine coping device we all employ in our efforts to avoid pain. The decision with which people in mourning are faced entails closing a vital part of their previous existences and opening a new phase of life—without the company, support, hopes, and aspirations so intimately linked with their loved ones. One must choose to treasure the loved one through the process of memory.

This may be the most difficult task for people in mourning. Even when the bereaved person has worked through accepting the reality of the loss, struggled through incapacitating feelings, abandoned the regrets, and is learning to live with the sadness and periods of loneliness and longing, there is still the pain of relinquishing the bonds with the loved one and choosing "to go on with one's life." It is, perhaps, like arriving at a turn in the road, waving, and turning to face the road ahead in the absence of the one from whom the survivor has been parted. Ultimately, one must choose to turn from preoccupation with the past to face and master the future.

Julie, a young mother, faced the reality of returning to full-time work following her husband's death. During one weekend, as she prepared to begin work on Monday, she anguished over the decision to place her three-year-old son in a nursery. Monday morning came, and she was unable to gather the resources to dress, take her child to the nursery, and set out for work. She called a friend, who helped with the morning chores and encouraged her to call her employer and explain her absence. The decision was made to defer her employment until the following day, thanks to an understanding employer. With the support of her friend, Julie spent Monday reviewing all the tasks for which she must now bear sole responsibility and expressing the pain of the loneliness she knew she must face. By Tuesday morning, she was ready to take her first tentative steps toward her new world, accompanied by the reality and pain of her bereavement.

When this task is completed, the most painful aspect of the mourning period is behind. There will continue to be days when tears fill the eyes and sadness overrules other feelings. But the grieving person is ready to take up his or her life and develop interests that will be pursued in the absence of the deceased loved one. On the other hand, the inability to complete this task marks the likelihood that the grieving person may continue cycling through the various aspects and experiences of the grieving process, instead of completing the work of mourning.

The decision to take up one's life in the absence of the loved one will often be expressed in the form of developing new relationships. This may be difficult for a surviving spouse whose patterns of daily living previously were fashioned, to a large degree, by the relationship with the former spouse. Presumably, they formed other relationships as a pair, made their plans in consultation with one another, participated in family events as parents or grandparents, and entertained their friends. That relationship ended with the death of the spouse. The survivor may now be inclined to withdraw from social contacts, rather than face the challenge of seeking or accepting new relationships. This may be a manifestation of self-pity and depression, perhaps out a sense of loyalty to the deceased. In the latter event, it appears that acceptance of the reality of the loss is incomplete. The alternative—developing new relationships—marks the readiness to turn the page and begin the next chapter of one's life.

Many bereaved people take their own paths as they work to be in touch with and accept—or resolve—their feelings. However, most bereaved people appear to work through grief more effectively when they have access to help and support from concerned family members or friends, resources such as pastors, hospice staff members, or grief groups sponsored by community self-help organizations.

A New Conceptual Model

Imagine that life is like walking a pathway. There are valleys and heights, exciting opportunities, obstructions—but generally, life consists in meeting daily responsibilities, and the path leads on ahead:

Figure 2

Suddenly, the death of a loved one intrudes, and life totally changes direction:

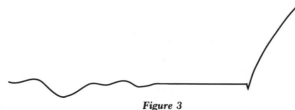

Figure 3

The person in mourning is faced with many tasks . . .

. . . accepting the reality of the loss;

. . . resolving anger if it present;

. . . coming to terms with feelings of regret, remorse, guilt, anxiety, and particularly sadness,

struggling to work through depression; and, finally,

. . . working beyond mourning toward resolution of grief and taking up one's life again in the absence of the loved one.

This work, with its various tasks, may be illustrated as in Figure 4. A seminar participant, looking at that diagram, sighed, "If only it were that simple!" But no diagram can do justice to the intensity of grief or its complex factors. We agreed that, at least, the diagram in Figure 5 is more true to the experience of most bereaved people.

Lengthening periods between the days of intense grief, and decreasing intensity in the level of grief are signals that the grieving person is moving toward resolution, including decisions to establish a new identity apart from the deceased, and even to enter new relationships. Because caregivers may oversimplify "the grief process" and are apt "psychologize" about "stages" rather than care for the bereaved person, I am ambivalent about reducing the process to two dimensional diagrams. They may infer stereotypical responses that assume a too-rigid notion of the grief process; and it has already been noted that grief is as unique as one's fingerprint. Nevertheless, such diagrams may serve to illustrate the often tortuous path of grief. With this reservation about the limitations of delineating this process, Figure 6 demonstrates the various tasks through which one person had to work. This figure illustrates that tasks may overlap, may be repeated, and do not necessarily occur in a particular order.

Granted its shortcomings, Figure 4 serves a further purpose. At any point in progress through grief work, the bereaved person may pause, or even be unable to move forward. In some cases, the person in mourning may be unable to accept the reality of the loved one's death, and failing to find emancipation from the deceased, wind into a tightening circle of denial (see Figure 7).

An article published in 1977 indicates how difficult it may be for some families to relinquish close physical ties to a member who has died:

> In a small suburban house near Detroit, the upstairs back bedroom has not been used in more than a year. The rumpled bed is unmade,

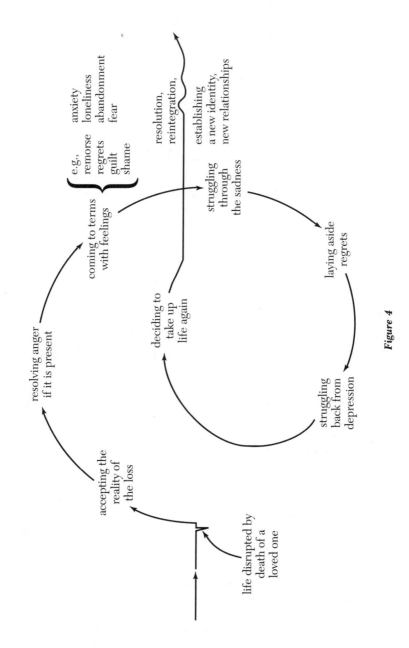

Figure 4

schoolbooks are stacked carelessly on the desk and a half-empty bottle of soda stands on the bureau. The room looks exactly as it did when the boy who lived there was killed in an automobile accident many months ago.

"His room will remain untouched as long as I live," says his mother. "This is how my son should be remembered."[30]

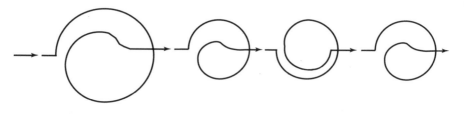

Figure 5

Memories are one of the most precious ways to treasure a family member who has died, and photos and other memorabilia are important aids in treasuring those memories and celebrating the life of the deceased. But the intensity with which one needs physical objects, and especially a decision to retain a room untouched indefinitely, may indicate inability to progress through healthy grieving to resolution.

Similarly, anger may be nursed in a vengeful manner toward a person who has died, or felt and expressed toward others—an employer, a family member, or, of course, God. There may indeed have been powerful reasons for anger—for example, toward a criminal who murdered the loved one, or the driver whose carelessness or drunkenness caused the death. If anger, even rage, is unremitting, one's life may become focused around this one emotion, inhibiting the grieving person from continuing through the tasks of mourning (see Figure 8).

Alternately, the mourner may be so consumed with regrets, loneliness, and longing that he or she experiences no relief from sadness and, perhaps, finds purpose in maintaining an excessive or permanent veil of mourning. Britain's Queen Victoria was one of the most grievous examples of such prolonged mourning. Her period of mourning for Prince Albert lasted from his death in 1861 until her death 40 years later (see Figure 9). Although not unusual according to reports of customary nineteenth-century mourning practices, the manifestations of the

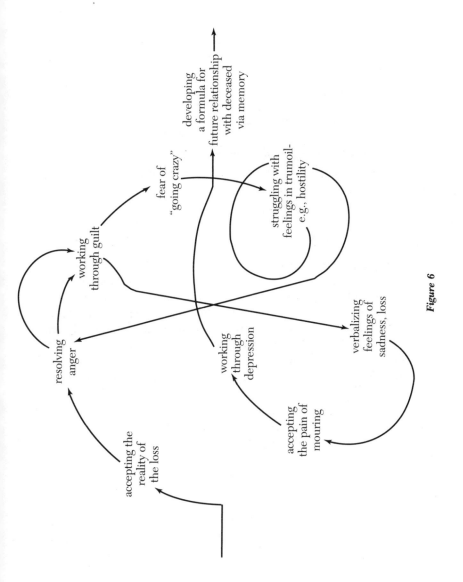

Figure 6

Queen's grief now seems exaggerated. In each of her homes, Albert's dressing room or study was kept as it had been, "even to the changing of linens, the daily replacement of towels and nightclothes, and—in the dressing rooms—the bringing of hot water for shaving each morning, and a scouring of the unused chamber pot. . . . Victoria's sole interest would be to embrace her grief."[31]

It is important to keep the distinction between sadness/pining and depression, although one may deepen into the other. When caregivers sense this is occurring, it is wise to obtain professional consultation. Worden warns that a caregiver working with a bereaved person may be able to recognize pathology which has been triggered by the loss. However, it may be necessary to make a professional referral. "It is important for grief counselors to recognize their limitations and to know when to refer a person for grief therapy or other psychotherapy."[32] The latter may be indicated when the grieving person's intensity of sadness or pining is unrelieved, or evokes anxiety, discomfort, or pain in family members, friends, or other caregivers.

blocking out
the reality

Figure 7

nursing
anger

Figure 8

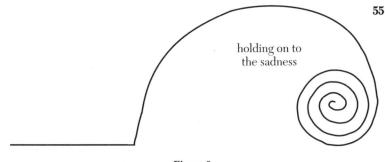

holding on to
the sadness

Figure 9

Jill K. Conway provides one of the most vivid contemporary descriptions of catastrophic, unresolved grief. In her account of her childhood at Coorain, a sheep station in western New South Wales, Conway tells of her father's tragic death during a destructive drought which began in 1940 and devastated the Australian outback until 1946. Her autobiography describes graphically the way the lives of grieving people may be destroyed when bereavement becomes a pattern of life and mourning extends year after year, accompanied by deteriorating physical and mental health. Conway's account of her mother's grief begins with the discovery of her father's body:

> After we went sleeplessly to bed, we heard a sound never heard before, the sound of my mother weeping inconsolably. It was a terrible and unforgettable sound. . . . [The following day], dispensing with all possibility of discussion, she announced that Barry and I were to stay with friends for a few days. She did not want us to see our father buried, believing that this would be too distressing for us. . . . I felt betrayed that I would not see him to his last rest.[33]

Thereafter, the book follows the interlocking paths of the griefs of mother and daughter during the harsh first months, then years, of bereavement. Physical manifestations of mourning ("she ate next to nothing, fell to weeping unexpectedly, and seemed much of the time in a trance. The effort expended in getting up and carrying on each day exhausted her") are joined with descriptions of her mother's deteriorating mental state:

> Her quest led her to small sects and groups of bereaved persons like herself who looked for insight from scrambled versions of Eastern wisdom, or sought comfort in contact with the spirits of the dead. She looked for tangible signs of the survival after death of those she loved even as she

studied great Oriental texts on surrendering the attachments of this world. My first awareness of her fallibility came from my recognition of the contradiction between these two desires, but the insight which this recognition prompted was indefinitely delayed by the fresh disasters which quickly turned my mother's suburban dream into an uninterrupted nightmare.[34]

The genesis of this new nightmare was the death of Conway's elder brother, Bob, who was killed in a car accident during a road race. Conway describes how her distraught mother was unable to recover from the multiple griefs of the drought, her husband's death, leaving Coorain to live in Sydney, her eldest son's death, and the frequent "smaller" griefs evoked by daily experiences of unwelcome changes in their life-style. Her own story is intertwined with that of her mother's story: "After my brother Bob's death, it seemed as though I had lost the capacity for emotional responses. Daily life was in black and white, like a badly made film. My trance-like state excluded music, feeling, color, desire. Although on the surface I was doing well, I was actually going through each day like an automaton."[35]

Conway leads her readers through her tortured pilgrimage from grief to her departure from Australia for the United States, a "rite of passage which was both a sentence and a release."[36] While Conway's mourning eased into a pervading but manageable grief, her mother was unable to make this transition, and we are left to speculate on the stark consequences of her inability to resolve her bereavement.

From Mourning to Grieving

Figure 4 has two further uses. First, it helps to distinguish mourning as a discrete function of grief—that is, as the initial phase of the grief process (see Figure 10):

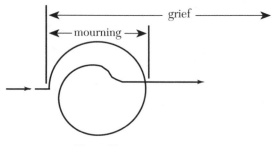

Figure 10

Second, it directs attention to the point at which the mourner emerges from this experience and begins the next task in rebuilding his or her life—the decision to establish a new identity, apart from the deceased (see Figure 11):

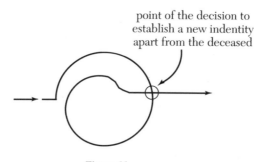

Figure 11

This point has been underidentified and therefore underemphasized in pastoral care of bereaved people. Ideally, and with few if any exceptions, the decision to take up one's life again needs to be made self-consciously. Caregivers will often be able to discern progress toward the point at which the bereaved person is ready to make this decision. The mourner's progress through the grief process will be effected in a healthier manner when this is addressed explicitly. This does not mean that grief is over, and sorrow and pining are ended. On the contrary, with the decision made to move beyond mourning, memories begin to become into focus more readily and may be enjoyed and treasured, although they often will be accompanied by sadness and longing. It does mean that bereavement is no longer incapacitating, and the possibility of new life is welcomed.

Yorick Spiegel calls this point in the grief process "the decision for life." He suggests that as insight into the reality of the loss grows stronger, the question as to whether it makes any sense to continue to live becomes more aggravating. In most cases, "the will to live succeeds, but how decisive and how fast this develops can vary a great deal. The decision to live certainly is a task in which the bereaved needs the help not only of the internalized good objects, but depends on outside support as well"[37] Working through grief is a task that is best socialized, yet at many points remains a very personal, individual struggle.

Poet C. S. Lewis described his own experience of mourning following his wife's death:

At first I was very afraid of going to places where H. and I had been happy—our favorite pub, our favorite wood. But I decided to do it at once—like sending a pilot up again as soon as possible after he's had a crash. Unexpectedly, it makes no difference. . . . Her absence is like the sky, spread over everything. . . .

You tell me "she goes on." But my heart and body are crying out, come back, come back. . . . The old life, the jokes, the drinks, the arguments, the love-making, the tiny, heart-breaking commonplace. . . . All that . . . is part of the past. . . .

And suddenly at the very moment when, so far, I mourned H. least, I remembered her best. Indeed it was something (almost) better than memory; an instantaneous, unanswerable impression. To say it was like a meeting would be going too far. Yet there was that in it which tempts one to use those words. It was as if the lifting of the sorrow removed a barrier.

Why has no one told me these things? How easily I might have misjudged another man in the same situation? I might have said, "He's got over it. He's forgotten his wife," when the truth was, "He remembers her better *because* he has partly got over it."

For some reason—the merciful good sense of God is the only one I can think of—I have stopped bothering about [my memory of H. and how false it might become]. And the remarkable thing is that since I stopped bothering about it, she seems to meet me everywhere.[38]

Lewis's graphic images are one person's efforts to share a personal grief. As caregivers and grievers, we have much to learn from one another. We are pilgrims, sharing a common path for a few steps of the journey, privileged to offer one another an arm on which to lean, a shoulder on which to weep. Bereavement is a process, or, as Lewis suggests, a universal and integral part of our experience of love: "It follows marriage as normally as marriage follows courtship or as autumn follows summer. It is not a truncation of the process but one of its phases; not the interruption of the dance, but the next figure."[39]

Caregivers may play a vital part in this transition. If the person in mourning appears to be blocked from moving from one task to another, the difficulty may be identified and support offered to facilitate the process. Progress in meeting tasks, working through them, and finally making the decision to move toward resolution, can be identified and affirmed amid tears and laughter.

Along the way, we have been hearing that *grief* is a generic term that encompasses bereavement, with its period of mourning, but extends into a myriad of experiences of loss and change. Sensing this in a kind of theoretical way is one thing; recognizing its vital importance for bereavement ministry is another matter. Chapter 3 will address and illustrate this relationship.

CHAPTER 3

Grief:
Our Constant Companion

*When sorrows come, they come not single spies,
but in battalions.*

HAMLET III.v.78

Griefs: Pressed Down and Running Over

Grief is far more pervasive and intrusive in our daily lives than most people are aware. Beginning with Lindemann's research in the early 1940s, researchers have noted that grief is likely to be evoked by any substantive loss. He cited the departure of a member of a family into the armed forces: "Separation in this case is not due to death but is under the threat of death."[1] Parkes extended this concept to include grief attributable to change: "In the ongoing flux of life [we] undergo many changes. Arriving, departing, growing, declining, achieving, failing—every change involves a loss and a gain."[2]

As noted before, Marris confirmed Parkes' findings, citing Fried's study of families displaced from their homes by an urban-renewal scheme. The majority of families experienced reactions of grief manifested in feelings of painful loss, continued longing, general depressive tone, and frequent symptoms of psychological, social, or somatic distress. Fried noted the active work required in adapting to the altered situation, the sense of helplessness, the occasional expressions of both direct and indirect anger, and tendencies to idealize the lost home. The grief reactions of some were intense and, at times, overwhelming.[3]

Thus, bereavement is the most obvious and widely recognized form of grief—but it is only one form grief may take. When presenting this concept in grief-education seminars, I draw a circle to represent the entire human experience of grief, of which bereavement is only one segment:[4]

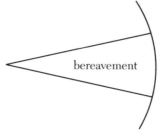

Figure 12

Divorce. Divorce also is usually accompanied by grief. During a discussion of the impact of grief in the schoolroom, a teacher stated, with considerable feeling, that "death is comparatively easy! It's over. You know where you are. But with my divorce, it never seems to be over. I go back through my grief every second weekend, when I pick up my children from their mother's home!" On one occasion, a seminar participant reported that he had gone through "a happy divorce"; most divorced people, I think, carry a grief with them through the years, either because of the bitterness which characterized the marriage and divorce proceedings, or a regret from which they find no release.

Anger or sadness evoked by divorce usually is felt by the spouse who feels wronged, and the children, who also suffer from the dissolution of the family.[5]

Retirement. Retirement similarly may be edged with grief. Bob reached retirement at the age of sixty-five, and within three months, informed his wife of forty-five years that he had filed for divorce. Devastated, she persuaded him to suspend proceedings until they had an opportunity to enter counseling. In the months that followed, I learned that Bob had been a hard-driving hardware salesman, topping the annual sales figures in the company for an unbroken twenty years—a remarkable feat. He identified a series of frustrations with his marriage, including relationships with his married daughter and son-in-law. Each seemed relatively minor, but at least he was making an effort to explore the sources of his restlessness. He called to ask if he could see me alone and we set the appointment.

He sat in silence for fifteen minutes, then poured out his story. Bob's father had died when he was eight. At eleven years of age, he secured a paper route to supplement his mother's income during the Depression. The following Christmas, his mother gave him a new bicycle as a mark of her thanks for his effort. He rode around the neighborhood for hours that Christmas Day, but at last was persuaded to allow his younger brother to ride his bike. His brother rode off but did not reappear, and they found him two blocks away, the bike crushed beneath a car. His brother received only minor scratches but the bike was damaged beyond repair.

Bob wept uncontrollably as he told his story. When he regained his composure, he told me he had never cried about the bicycle until that moment. He knew his mother could not afford to replace the bike, so he had swallowed his tears. He had worked his way through high school and college, joined the wholesale hardware company for which he had worked all his life, and created sales records year after year.

In subsequent sessions, he was able to recognize the extent to which he had invested all his energies in his education and subsequent job successes, deferring his grief and anger—not only over the loss of his bicycle, but over his loss of his relationship with his father. This latter aspect he was able to explore only with great hesitation. He then was also able to grieve over his retirement. He talked with some pain about how he missed his work and office contacts. Painfully, he began to work through that grief with his wife and, together, plan a very full retirement.

Retirement can be a more painful transition than some other life changes, Evelyn and James Whitehead note:

> At retirement, what we are giving up (one's personal and social identity as a worker) is often much clearer than what it is we will gain (since our culture's image and expectations of postretirement life are vague and often negative). Even in its ambiguity, however, retirement can mark a movement into a new stage of personality expansion, [but] with most of life behind us, we face the question of its significance. This can be an anxious question.[6]

Forced Retirement. Forced retirement may add another measure of grief. Tom Peterson was called to the personnel office, where the vice-president for personnel informed him that the decision had been made to offer him early retirement. It soon emerged that it was not so much an offer as a firm decision. Tom had started work in the plant at the age of twenty, and now at fifty-eight, could not believe they would treat him like this. He was not ready to retire—he still had years to work. As the decision sank in, he began to bluster, reminding them of his unblemished record and his commitment to the firm over the years. His anger extended over the ensuing weeks. He suggested that there might be a place in the plant where he could continue working on a part-time basis and utilize his long experience in his field. That was rejected, and Tom became more morose, then depressed. He carried a feeling of injustice with him and refused a party in his honor on his last day at work.

Relocation or Moving. The Jones family moved recently from deep in the "snow belt" to South Texas. The new family expressed their pleasure that, at last, they had been able to escape wintry snow banks. Their neighbors welcomed them to the sunny South, helping them to settle in. Within three months, however, Mrs. Jones seemed to her neighbors to be depressed and less inclined to socialize with other families. Her reaction to moving is not unusual. She was missing family and friends from her previous neighborhood, church activities in which she had participated, and even the house itself, in which she had spent the first years of her marriage. The Texas neighborhood looked different from the familiar Northeast clapboard houses, and Texans were different, too. She felt as if her roots had been torn up—as indeed, in a sense, they had been.

Mrs. Jones was grieving for her previous life-style, with its familiar, comfortable patterns. She may or may not ultimately settle in her new home and neighborhood, depending on the extent to which she is able—or prepared—to cut the intimate ties she has preserved in her mind with her previous home, and choose to make a new life for herself and her family in Texas. As with bereavement, it is a turning point in her life—a choice she must make.

Some "migrants" find the task too difficult and return to their former homes. For example, many families that had moved from Britain to Australia in the postwar migration of the 1950s found Australia a land of opportunities and quickly adjusted to a very different life from that which they had left. Contacts with family members in Britain were maintained through mail and occasional phone calls. Other families were so home-sick—that is, grieved so deeply for all they had left behind, that within months of arrival they had packed and returned to Britain.

Marris notes that relocation is not necessarily accompanied by grief:

> Even changes which require a radical reorientation of life need not be disruptive, if they fulfill a purpose already pressing for expression. These changes are represented in the normal process of growing up. They are characteristically preceded by boredom and restlessness, as new concerns, not yet articulated or focussed, begin to divest the present of importance . . . exposing the triviality of habitual expectations and setting people on a new adventure.[7]

He warns, however, that moving or taking a new job may involve the sacrifice of familiar relationships with neighbors, colleagues, a community whose interest one shared; though the new job or house may be better, that does not overcome the need to mourn, at least a little, for the loss.

Unemployment. Like many other events that may be experienced as traumatic, unemployment often is grievous to employees and their families. Plant closings in the steel industry in Pennsylvania during the 1970s resulted in widespread unemployment, accompanied by deeply felt grief. Steelworkers felt betrayed—and robbed—by company managements and, beyond them, by banks. Men and women who wanted to work, but could not, saw their homes repossessed. Children became accustomed to making do on less, as family incomes shrank. Families were forced to apply for welfare benefits, losing their pride in the process. Trust in the basic elements of societal management was forfeited. Grief was piled upon grief.[8]

As the recession of the 1970s and the 1980s repeats in the 1990s, people whose lives have not been interrupted by forced unemployment may find it difficult to comprehend the grief that is evidenced, not only by blue-collar workers and their families but by white-collar workers as well. Similarly, only those who have experienced personal or business bankruptcy can tell of a grief that evokes a sense of failure and loss of self-esteem and self-identity.

Change of Job. Changing jobs is an instance of what Marris terms "a process of major reconstruction." As in other areas of grief, he is not so much concerned with the circumstances that demand change (though it should be noted that these circumstances may contribute to, or exacerbate the intensity of, grief), but with the processes by which one works through the feeling of loss: The more radical the changes which evolve, the more important it is to recognize the element of grief in a major life change.[9]

Surgical Amputation. Mastectomy, hysterectomy, amputation of one's leg (whether one is a sixty-nine-year-old brittle diabetic or a nineteen-year-old motorcyclist) or, for that matter, any intrusive surgical procedure which threatens one's life or changes one's self-image, is likely to evoke grief. Much attention has been given to "body image" and the impact of perceived change in self-image on psychological health. Parkes described the reaction to loss of a limb following amputation, reporting that amputees showed a grief response, including a typical period of shock and numbness, restless pining, preoccupation with thoughts of the loss, visual images of the lost limb and a sense of its presence.

He noted coping devices—for example, difficulty in accepting the reality of the loss and avoidance of reminders. He compared the responses of amputees to those of recently bereaved widows and found that the grief exhibited by amputees tended to remain intense during the first year, whereas that of widows tended to abate over the same period.[10]

As with other traumatic losses and changes, the responses of people who have suffered physical trauma very widely. Some people seem to be able to accept their respective realities, work through any anger evoked by the loss, struggle through regrets and depressive periods, and move forward with confidence and courage. Others may be devastated by disability and grieve unremittingly their loss or life change.[11] This is particularly evident in the case of spinal injuries.

Paraplegia or Quadriplegia.[12] I received a letter recently which enclosed reproductions of landscapes painted by a person with quadriplegia, who, the letter informed me, paints with a brush held between her teeth. I am reluctant to consign that appeal to the trashbasket with other requests for charitable gifts (one cannot respond favorably to every request!). For if a person has worked through grief evoked by such a trauma, he or she merits acclamation from those of us who have not been tested in such a manner. Of course, regardless of the degree to which they have triumphed over adversity, people whose lives have been disrupted by catastrophic loss or change represent a claim on our compassion.

Having a Disability. From the back of the audience, seventy-four-year-old Bill Thomas called out, "Going blind." We were discussing sources of grief, and suddenly it wasn't just an exercise, a theoretical model. Bill shared his grief with us. "Legally blind," they had said to him, and they took away his driver's license. Losing the license was almost as bad as losing his sight, he told us.

My nine-year-old grandson, Jason, has profound deafness, his hearing destroyed by pneumococcal meningitis at the age of thirteen months—that is, at the prelingual stage. He is learning oral speech, and though he has a disability, he is a bright, happy boy. But he will never hear a Beethoven sonata, a Bach chorale, or the "Hallelujah Chorus." In the first draft of this chapter I added that I grieved a loss of which Jason was not even aware.

This summer, however, Jason came to spend two weeks with us. We called his parents from time to time, to assure them Jason was missing them, but was quite happy where he was! Jason, aware we were talking by phone with his mom and dad, said quickly: "Mandy can talk on the phone. But I can't. I'm deaf." Sometimes, the grief strikes, like a knife to the heart, when one is least prepared. . . .

Griefs Related to Procreation. A birth anticipated with joy may still be accompanied by moments of ambivalence in which grief may be included. In Britain, the term *postpartum insanity (postpartum blues* sounds less threatening) refers to the syndrome of sadness or depression which may afflict mothers of neonates, but in which fathers may also participate. The birth of the baby, however happily expected, is followed by changes in relationships, schedules, responsibilities, and expectations, all of which may represent significant rearrangements in the life of each family member. And with change lies the potential for grief. That the inability to conceive children, an unwanted pregnancy, or an abortion (even when acceptable to both mother and father) usually will be experienced as griefs needs little elaboration.

Birth of a Child with a Disability. Physicians refer to some mothers of newborns with physical or mental impairments as "doctor-hoppers," because they move from one pediatrician to another, hoping to find a doctor who will reinforce their denial of the impairment. It is difficult for a parent of healthy children to imagine the pain of parents whose children are born with catastrophic diseases or disabilities. Most parents anticipating a birth may be anxious, hoping for a "perfect" child—what father has not counted his baby's toes! One has only to sit with parents or grandparents in the waiting area of a neonatal intensive-care unit to gauge the depth of sorrow, dismay, or denial—grief—which overwhelms a family when their fondest hopes and dreams have been swept aside by the reality of a less-than-perfect newborn.

The Empty Nest Syndrome. The Johnsons have an empty bird's nest tacked to their front door! It is a little like those notices posted on front lawns: "It's a girl!" We like to share our joys, I guess. And for some parents, the departure of the last child from home seems like a time for celebration. One's role as a parent of dependent children has been fulfilled, and now one can get on with the rest of one's life, unencumbered by daily chores like getting the offspring out of the house in time for school, car-pooling a bunch of their peers, or attending every Little League baseball game. Surprisingly, perhaps, some parents experience "a little grief" with the departure of the last child to college or marriage. I understand that the *return* of a child to an "empty nest" may also be an occasion for grief! Either way, it represents a major shift in daily activities, as well as marking a deeper issue: It usually coincides with mid-life crisis.

Mid-life Crisis. I have a friend who once urged me never to use the term mid-life *crisis*. He maintained that mid-life should always be referred to as mid-life *opportunity*. Only he wasn't at that stage at the time. The term *menopause* used to be restricted to women, until psychologists began to talk about male menopause. For many mid-life adults, the late forties and early fifties mark a period of stress. If the stage of life characterized by Erikson as "generativity vs. stagnation" is accompanied by unfulfilled plans and thwarted aspirations, it may be an occasion for grief. As Shakespeare noted:

> There is a tide in the affairs of men
> Which, taken at the flood, leads on to fortune;
> Omitted, all the voyage of their life

Is bound in shallows and miseries.
On such a full sea are we now afloat;
And we must take the current when it serves,
Or lose our ventures.
                              Julius Caesar IV.iii.218-24

Significant changes may occur—children leave home, job security may be threatened, or a long-treasured hope that is now illusive may be abandoned—which leave the mid-lifer disappointed and frustrated. Physical activities may be impaired as aging is grudgingly acknowledged. Some men may deal with the threat through behaviors described by observers as second childhood. Others may experience depression. My friend is right. For some people, life is rich with opportunities, and mid-life is just one of them; yet for others, the philosopher's words are painfully real: "Change is not made without inconvenience, even from worse to better!"[13]

Aging. Over all mid-life crises, great or small, hangs the "specter of aging and death." William Hulme uses this term in his volume *Mid-Life Crises*, reminding his readers that, at mid-life, they are now at a time they once considered old—that is, the second half of life. Hulme suggests that the same sense of aloneness that may cause distress in adolescents may recur at mid-life, and be just as frightening, because it is often accompanied by new threats: Our bodies are older and showing the weight of our years, reminding us that we are drawing closer to the end of life.[14]

Aging, of which earlier life-passages were premonitions, usually refers to the years beyond sixty—the retirement period. Though I remember going through this exercise with a group of junior-high students, one of whom, wise beyond his years, volunteered "getting old" as a grief experience. As with other potentially threatening experiences, we mask our anxieties by using euphemisms like "senior citizens" (now more often just "seniors"), "elders," or Gray Panthers.

Andrew and Judith Lester write for children of aging parents, noting that older people often must deal with loss of bodily functions, skin texture, hearing, and vision: "Loss and grief are constant companions of aging individuals. They face changes in life characterized by words and phrases such as 'fading,' 'impairment,' 'slowed-down,' 'gone,' 'used to,' and 'when I was your age.' . . . It is normal for our parents to grieve over these losses."[15]

Loss of Hopes and Dreams. We often must face disappointments during our lives—in fact, they can be daily occurrences. Most of the time when we are hurt, angry, regretful, or sad, we pick ourselves up and go on. When the loss is more intense, moments of grief may lengthen into days, years, or last a lifetime. Failure to receive an expected promotion, learning one's child is using drugs, betrayal by a friend, or failure to achieve anticipated goals may be grieved for extended periods. In a journal article with that title, J. Grayson draws attention to "Grief Reaction to the Relinquishing of Unfulfilled Wishes."[16] He noted that whereas some people accept what realistically can be fulfilled, others experience sadness, anger, or guilt as they relinquish hopes critical to resolution of their dreams.

Damage to Property. Natural disasters often result in extensive damage to property, apart altogether from frequent loss of life. In these events, loss and grief are experienced not only at the individual level, but often at community and even national and international levels. The 1988 fires in Yellowstone National Park, for example, grieved many people who were devastated by the damage to this natural resource. Anger was heaped upon the Park Service for its apparently gross error in permitting fires caused by natural events (e.g., lightning) to burn uncontrolled. South Carolina families suffering as a result of Hurricane Hugo in 1989, and families in Florida, Louisiana, and Hawaii after hurricanes Andrew and Iniki in 1992, will continue to grieve the loss of homes and disruption of their lives long after the rest of the country has relegated these storms to past history.

Loss of Property. Alma mislaid her favorite pair of shoes. It seemed so ridiculous; they couldn't just disappear. They must be somewhere in the apartment. The children all claimed they had not touched the shoes. Two years later, Alma still looks for them in boxes among which she has searched more than once. She misses these shoes.

Beth described how she first missed the diamond from her engagement ring when she returned from the store. She called the manager of the supermarket, but no one had handed in a diamond. She hurried back to the store, looking along every aisle where she had shopped, but to no avail. She remembered that as she had returned from the store the car window was lowered, and she had rested her arm along the door frame. Perhaps the vibration had shaken the stone loose. She drove home slowly, looking along the side of the streets she always used, hoping to see the glint of sunlight from her diamond. She wept as she told the group that her loss had occurred five years previously, and she still looks for the diamond each time she drives home from the store.

Damage to one's home through fire, flood, mud slide, earthquake, or storm may result in the loss of personal possessions, and perhaps of the entire home. People faced with such catastrophic losses may grieve less over the loss of the structure ("It can be replaced") than of personal belongings like family photographs or keepsakes which have been in the family over the generations and can never be restored or replaced.

The intensity of our responses to personal loss depends upon the value *we* have invested in the lost object, regardless of whether others think the loss significant. The more intense the "bonds" we have forged with an object, the greater will be the sense of loss, and therefore the grief that is likely to accompany it. When five-year-old Bobby loses his favorite toy and cries inconsolably, he is unlikely to be comforted when his father responds, "Why are you so upset—it was broken, anyway!" or "We can always buy another one." As adults, we know how little we are comforted when others respond in similar vein—for example, "Well, it was overdue for the trash," or "I don't understand why you are making such a fuss over it!"

The attachment of children to a blanket or other soft object has entered into folklore via Charles Schultz's Linus. In a typical episode, Lucy declares that the "blanket burning" has begun: "As I toss your blanket into the trash burner, your insecurities are symbolically destroyed forever!"

Linus watches unbelievingly, his hair standing on end, as Lucy drops the treasured object into the burner and says, "There! You are now free from the terrible hold it once had on you. . . . You are a new person!"

But the bereft Linus is attached to his blanket; he responds with a terrifying screech of pain—"AAUGHH!" followed by a burst of anger: "GIVE ME BACK THAT BLANKET! No one is going to cure me of ANYthing! Who are YOU to tell me what to do? Who is GRAMMA to tell me what to do? When MOM tells me it's time to stop dragging this blanket around, then I'll do it, but it's no one else's business, DO YOU HEAR?"

Charlie Brown responds with a cheer, and Lucy snaps, "Oh, shut up!" as Linus recovers and cuddles his blanket. Restitution has occurred, and Linus's grief is resolved.

John Bowlby states that such attachments arise because of a need for security. Usually, of course, loved objects are replaced by loved people, and the resulting attachments may last a lifetime. They represent a bulwark against anxiety as long as they remain intact. But with the absence—or death—of the person to whom one has been attached, anxiety grows into a psychic pain often expressed as an emotional protest. Bowlby discounts psychoanalytic theories that attachment behavior that is active throughout life is indicative either of pathology or of regression to immature behavior.[17] Bowlby suggests that death of a loved person is as traumatic psychologically as being severely wounded or burned is physiologically. The processes of mourning are not unlike those of healing: "They may take a course that leads in time to more or less complete restoration of function, namely, to a renewal of the capacity to make and maintain love relationships; or they may take a course that leaves this function impaired to a greater or lesser degree."[18]

Personal Violation. The burglary of one's home, people have told me, is a grief experience marked by initial shock, numbness, and disbelief, quickly followed by anger/rage, "if onlys" (regrets), and depressive feelings, all of which are often related to the sense of having been violated—not just violation of privacy, but of security and of items with deeply personal meaning and significance. The "home" is now just a "house." Robbery of one's person-being mugged—is also an affront likely to be grieved.

The ultimate violation of one's person, rape, is a deeply felt grief for the person violated and for other family members. Similarly, spouse and child abuse are actions which destroy aspects of personhood at the core of the victim's being: trust in adults; threat of perceived loss of self-esteem and self-worth, of security, and of the ability to enjoy fundamental aspects of personal growth, such as development of mature and satisfying relationships—griefs too numerous to list and, perhaps, too intense to confront directly.

Returning to the model of the circle with its many segments, representing the global nature of grief, we begin to recognize that we could add more and more segments as the awareness of group members expands.

Grief in one form or another emerges as a constant companion in our daily lives, for life consists of constant loss and change. Yet while from early childhood we may have been conditioned to respond to change,

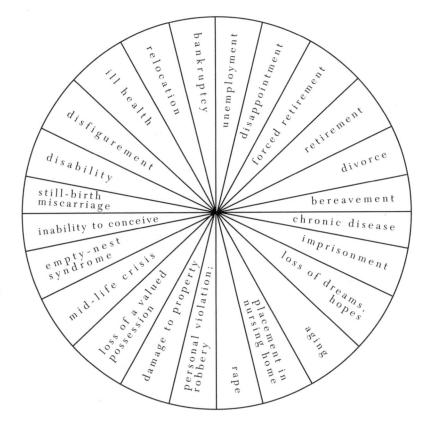

Figure 13

we rarely face its consequences at a cognitive level. Management of grief is not taught in our schools, and most adults are often slow to recognize that they are grieving in respect to specific life changes or other losses.

During a seminar with an adult group, a sixty-four-year-old member interrupted the session with a gasp: "Thank goodness, I am in grief." We asked Ruth to explain. She told us that she and her husband had lived in Houston until sixteen years ago. Their two teenage boys were in high school, and their lives could not have been happier or more settled. John's company announced that a new office was to be opened in Corpus Christi and offered the managership to John. Ruth urged him not to accept it—she did not want to live at the ends of the world for anyone, even John. It was just too big a sacrifice to make.

John was informed that if he did not take the position, he would lose any opportunity for promotion. He moved to Corpus, but Ruth refused to go. During the first twelve months, he commuted every third weekend to spend time with Ruth and the boys in Houston. By the end of that first year, he was fed up, and pressed Ruth to move.

> I did so grudgingly, because I knew I wouldn't like Corpus. Well, I didn't! It was as bad as I knew it would be. I guess I made sure of that. By the end of the year, though, I had made a few friends, joined a congregation, and begun to put down roots. The boys liked their new schools, made friends quickly, and life settled down again. In fact, the past fourteen years have been the happiest years of our lives. Three months ago, when John retired, we moved back to Houston.

With a change in her voice, Ruth continued: "For the past three months, I have been afraid I was going crazy. Thank goodness it is just grief!" She described how, in the first days in their Houston home, while John was reading the paper over coffee after breakfast, she would dial her friend, Betty (she and Betty had called each other most mornings after their husbands left for work). The phone was answered by a person whose voice she did not recognize. She asked for Betty, only to be informed there was no Betty at that number. Confused, she would redial Betty's number carefully, but with the same result. Only then did she remember that she now lived in Houston, and Betty was in Corpus Christi, a long-distance call away.

When on these occasions she burst into tears, it was John's turn to be confused. He grew increasingly impatient with her as these episodes recurred, asking her more than once: "Are you going crazy?" Ruth told us she was afraid she was! She expressed both her relief that she was not going crazy and her wish that someone had been there to help her understand that the move from Corpus Christi to Houston would be accompanied not only by gratification but by grief: "If I had known that, it would not have been so scary!"

Ruth's story relates to grief evoked by moving, but it is typical of almost any experience of loss or change—if accompanying grief is unrecognized, it can be confusing, even unnerving. The consequence may be even more devastating when grief episodes pile up, unrecognized by either sufferer or family members or friends. The following fictional case study illustrates and emphasizes this concern.

John and Mary Gibson: A Case Study

John and Mary Gibson were married in Flint in 1964.[19] John had graduated with an engineering degree and was employed in an auto plant. Mary had not completed her undergraduate degree in library science because of her first pregnancy and their decision that she would care for Elizabeth, their first child, then John, Jr., and their third child, Jimmy.

Throughout 1984, John was restless. Age forty-four, he longed to own his own company; he was tired of working for other bosses. By 1987, he had overcome Mary's reluctance and her resistance to using their savings, and launched Gibson Enterprises, Inc. His confidence in his business and engineering skills was borne out in the first two years. The business prospered and the family began to appreciate their new life-style. The only item missing was the savings account, for all profits were reinvested in the company. But that would change, given time. John, Jr. bought his first car, and they began to talk about a lakeside summer house.

Their daughter, Elizabeth, was married, and her husband, Bill, was as much a part of the family as John, Jr., and Jimmy. Mary was fond of telling Elizabeth that she had chosen well. When their first grandchild was born, Mary wondered if it was right—or safe—to be so happy.

John was caught by surprise by the recession in the auto industry. He lost accounts despite his close relationships with people in his old company. He struggled on for a few months, but in September 1989, was forced to take Chapter 11 protection; he was bankrupt, and there were no family savings to serve as a cushion. John was not rehired by his previous company—the labor market was choked by a surplus of engineers. The first asset to be liquidated (that was how John put it) was John, Jr.,'s car. They needed the cash, but Jr. was hurting; a nineteen-year-old without wheels is in grief. Other sacrifices followed, leading the family deeper into grief. John remained at home, idle. Mary now experienced periods of bitterness and anger. She wished she had persisted in her efforts to keep part of the savings account in reserve. She could not say "I told you so"—she doubted she could do so without expressing her anger, her deep sense of insecurity, and her fears, and that would only leave John more depressed.

Mary struggled to keep the family together. She sensed John was unable to cope with her grief as well as his own, and she could not afford to plunge him further into his melancholy state. She began to lose confidence in John and in herself. Often unable to sleep, she wondered what had happened to the happy world she had built in her imagination, when things had been different and the future had seemed so rosy. Now, her dreams had died.

In December, as they looked forward to a dreary Christmas, John read, in an engineering journal, an advertisement for a chief engineer in a plant in Fort Myers, Florida. He phoned to ask for details, was called for an interview, and hired enthusiastically by the management. By mid-January 1990, the Gibsons were settled in their new home. The boys were ecstatic over the combination of Florida sun, beaches, and quickly acquired surf skis. John was pleased with his new opportunity. He did not talk to Mary about it, but ideas of building up the new concern as a basis to starting out on his own again were already forming. Mary kept her feelings to herself. She was pleased for John and comforted by the boys' enthusiasm. But she missed the closeness to her parents in Flint, and her congregational ties. More than anything, she missed Elizabeth, Bill, and her grandsons. Mary grieved silently.

Three months after settling in Fort Myers, Elizabeth called from Flint to tell her parents she was filing for divorce. For a startled moment, Mary and John thought she was teasing them. They were stunned to realize she was serious, and their surprise turned to anger. Furious, they accused their daughter of stupidity in abandoning Bill—where would she ever find another husband so devoted to her and the children? Didn't she realize that Bill was one of the family? Had she thought of the impact on the children? No problem is so great that it cannot be solved; surely if they needed counseling, it was available. Elizabeth would not listen to her parents, but indicated she would need to stay with them "for a while." They informed her that if she was going to make such a thoughtless decision, she had better stay in Flint until she came to her senses, and the conversation was ended. The relationship was not healed in the following months.

John's leadership in the new plant was appreciated greatly by the owners, and much of the success of the new concern through 1990 was due to his efforts. The family had joined First Church, and Mary began to play an active part in the PTA at the boys' school. The boys seemed settled, and, but for the breach in their relationship with Elizabeth, their world was beginning to feel whole again. On September 14, Mary received a call from the plant. John was having chest pains and an ambulance had been called. The manager suggested that Mary drive straight to the hospital. John died from a heart attack two days later.

The Course of Grief During the First Twelve Months

There are no means by which one can specify the duration of mourning. Any attempt to indicate even an approximate length of bereavement fails to take account of individual differences. Spiegel notes that an individual's grief process is unpredictable, "because the forms of ties that bound the bereaved with the dead person are too various; the environment reacts very differently and the resources and coping mechanisms available to the bereaved change from person to person."[20] Davidson suggests that most people require up to two years before they are ready to take up a normal life after a major loss.[21] Davidson's point is not that either a one- or two-year period is somehow mandatory, but that the needs of people in mourning endure far longer than the surrounding community has assumed, and may extend for two years or even longer. A parent grieving the death of a child may take much longer than two years, and a surviving spouse may adapt effectively to his or her loss in considerably less time, depending on the person and the circumstances of the spouse's death.

Nevertheless, special attention must be given to the course of grief during the first year of bereavement. The manner in which grief work is undertaken may determine the degree of resolution that ultimately will be achieved.

Let us imagine we can draw a graph of the course "normal" grief is likely to take in the first year of mourning. First, grief does *not* subside in some mathematically simple form (see Figure 14).

intensity of mourning

duration of mourning

Figure 14

For most people, the course grief follows is related to the daily, weekly, and monthly times and events that are linked irrevocably to the deceased. On how many days in the first year will the grieving person be reminded of his or her loss? Ask a person in grief, and the answer will be "365": "Every day at five o'clock; that is when he (or she) came home from work." Or, "At 3:00 in the afternoon, when I hear the children on their way home from school." Widows or widowers may respond: "Every Sunday at two o'clock."

If we ask on which days in the year Mary is likely to face her sharpest grief, the issue becomes more personal, yet it is not difficult to imagine her "worst" days and sketch the course of her grief: family birthdays, the first wedding anniversary since John's death, Mother's Day and Father's Day, significant holidays, dates of events which carry significance for Mary and, of course, the first anniversary of John's death. Such days can "bring back the entire weight of grief," writes Spiegel, even though the periods of most intense pain may be shorter, fade faster, and occur less frequently.[22] The following "picture" (Figure 15) represents more accurately the course of "normal" grief:

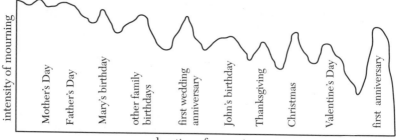

Figure 15

Mary's Management of Her Own Grief. The intensity of grief evoked by the death of a loved one is correlated highly with the intensity of the bonds that existed between survivors and the deceased.[23] This is expressed popularly in such terms as "Grief is the pain of severed love."[24] Mary's relationship with John had been loving and sustaining, and her anguish was correspondingly profound. As she sought to cope with her bereavement, however, her inability to complete the work of mourning was related directly to pain compounded by other sources of grief.

Her ambivalence over their decision to invest all their savings, including John's life-insurance policy, in his business venture led to feelings of betrayal and bitterness; these were alleviated with the apparent success they had enjoyed so briefly, but returned with the bankruptcy. This grief was deepened by her loss of confidence in John as the consequences of the loss of financial security burst upon her. She carried these griefs with her to Florida. The family's relocation to Fort Myers was accompanied by a sense of renewal in John and the two boys, but for Mary, it meant the loss of the familiar, of her daily contacts with Elizabeth, Bill, and her two grandchildren, and of the home that meant so much to her. These losses, in turn, paled in the face of Elizabeth's decision to divorce Bill and the subsequent breach in her relationship with Mary and John, a grief surpassed only by that evoked by John's death.

Mary was thus already reeling from a mounting burden of grief when John died, but people outside the immediate family circle were only dimly aware of her needs. She and John had not shared the stories of their losses with the few friends they made in Fort Myers. After all, bankruptcy and then Elizabeth's inexplicable divorce were hardly events in which they took pride. At the moment when she was most in need of the support system she had known in Flint—her family, congregation, and circle of friends—she felt isolated and alone. As the weeks passed, her isolation and loneliness and periods of depression deepened.

People who are able to work through grief with little or no external support are exceptions to a general rule; most of us need the support of others—family, friends, or a support group—in order to resolve our griefs and make the "decision for life" (see Figure 11 above). People usually are able to work through grief effectively if they have someone who is ready to sit and listen to their stories of loss and anguish. Indeed, most mourners actively seek what I term story-listeners, intuitively knowing they need to share their stories as the first step toward liberation from the restraining bonds of mourning.

Mary will be helped to work through her grief if she is able to achieve a balance between conserving moments of privacy, in which she does her own "grief work," and using opportunities to make her grief "public." I noted, in *Working Through Your Grief*, that "one of the most important ways in which you can complete the task of grieving is to let your grief become 'public' rather than keeping it locked away inside you. The public with which you choose to share your anguish may be just one or two people. But if you have someone with whom you feel secure, and can share with that person the depth of your loss, you will be comforted and strengthened."[25]

Many authors and lecturers, however, address grief work as if it were an individual effort. Self-help books which address the mourner personally, as if all that is needed is an understanding of the grief process and the personal strength to tread its lonely paths, may mislead their readers. Spiegel warns that grief is not only a personal event; it takes place within a network of relationships:

> The bereaved must newly create his relationships to the deceased *and his environment;* however, his environment as well as himself is affected by such a change in status. According to the concept of crisis theory, the grief process can be understood as interaction process between a psycho-social burden and an individual. Although it takes place in this social "arena," the crisis situation still appears to be very much the problem of the *individual.* The need for a more comprehensive concept is obvious (emphasis added).[26]

In communities in the United States, opportunities are widely available for bereaved people to "publicize" grief. Self-help groups such as The Compassionate Friends (a national program that provides support to bereaved parents), and hospice organizations that provide community-based grief-support groups, exist in most large cities and in many smaller communities. Local congregations may also facilitate development of such programs, for the church and synagogue, more than any other societal unit, are faced not only with the task of helping people in grief, but traditionally have been perceived as *the* locus for such support. Sadly, it is often provided only on a nominal basis. In most communities, Mary is unlikely to receive the support she needs from her congregation. This concern is addressed in the next chapter.

CHAPTER 4

Developing
a Grief Ministry

Give sorrow words: the grief that does not speak
Whispers the o'er fraught heart, and bids it break.
MACBETH IV.iii.208

The Congregation's Response to Mary's Grief

Despite the confidence of congregational leaders that they provide adequate continuing grief ministry in the months that follow the funeral, that perception is not shared by many grieving families. Many report that they felt overlooked and forgotten within a few days of the family member's death and funeral. The needs of Mary and her family will be examined in light of this concern.

Many bereaved people have responded to the question, "How long after the funeral were you aware of support from within your congregation?" with this response: "The care stopped with the casseroles." This does not mean literally that all support ministry was withdrawn, and the retort may be saying more about the capacity of the person in grief to accept support than about the quality or duration of the care offered. Yet the response is too widespread to be ignored and is confirmed by the responses of the sample of clergy and laypeople with whom I have reviewed this issue.

In presenting the Gibson study to clergy during the SCI "Working Through Your Grief" seminars, three questions were posed in an attempt to discern the patterns of grief ministry in congregations across the country:

1. In how many congregations will Mary receive some measure of grief support on the first wedding anniversary following John's death?
2. In how many congregations will Mary receive pastoral support on the first anniversary of John's death?
3. In how many congregations will John, Jr., and Jimmy receive grief ministry during the first year.

Clergy and lay responses alike indicated that less than 3 percent of their congregations customarily follow through with these basic ministries. That is, in 97 percent of congregations, Mary and her family would receive only nominal support, and there is no self-conscious, intentional effort to focus pastoral care around the family's grief-needs on occasions during the first year, when those needs are likely to be most intense. Yet on days like wedding anniversaries, family birthdays, and especially the first anniversary of a family member's death, grief is real and intense. Pastoral support is not only warranted, but may be the critical factor which determines whether the individual or family moves toward resolution—or fails to do so. On the basis of the model (see Figure 15 above), there are *at least* ten to twelve days during the first year of grief when Mary should be supported by her congregation's care.

In one of the grief seminars, a pastor jumped to his feet and shouted from the back of the hall: "You are making me very angry!" With twenty funerals each year, he said there was no way he could add another two hundred additional grief visits to his already overloaded schedule. That left him feeling guilty, he said, and angry with me for implying he was not fulfilling his ministry. I responded that I had neither stated nor implied that he himself should undertake these visits. He complained that there was no other person who could do so. When I inquired whether there were not laypeople who, if not already prepared, could be trained to provide this ministry—for that is where the task should lie in the congregation—he quietly resumed his seat. His unspoken answer was eloquent: He had not seen laypeople as ministers to people in grief.

Planning for Grief Ministry in the Congregation

Now take our hypothetical congregation, First Church. There are approximately twelve congregant deaths each year—that is, each month a new family enters the first year of grief. The pastoral ministry program is thus faced with a minimum of 100 to 150 grief visits each year which should be incorporated into the overall ministry of the congregation. First Church will need to train a group of lay pastoral ministers to focus on care of families in their first year of bereavement, and provide follow-up care beyond the first year when indicated. In addition, First Church should also institute a Grief-support Group, in which bereaved members may share their experiences in a small-group setting.

Such ministry is possibly only when using the gifts of lay ministers. I have argued elsewhere that pastoral care is the responsibility not of the clergy but of the congregation.[1] That is, grief support, as one of the primary focuses of congregational pastoral care, is one of the ministries for which lay people are gifted, and therefore to which they are called.

With the endorsement of the parish council, the pastoral staff of First Church invited recently bereaved members to assist in planning the grief-support ministry.[2] Members were invited personally by phone call, followed by a letter, to meet for dinner at the church. The staff explained that the purpose of the meeting and discussion was to examine the effectiveness of the congregation's grief ministry to its members, and to identify ways the congregation could strengthen its grief-support ministry. They were asked to share . . .

. . . whether they had received adequate support in their bereavement;

. . . which (if any) of their needs were not met;

. . . what aspects of grief ministry were the greatest help;

. . . what suggestions they might have for developing effective grief ministry.

During the meeting, the pastoral staff provided opportunity for "storytelling." Grieving members shared bereavement experiences as they reviewed the existing ministry and planned for the future.

The pastoral staff's review of grief ministry at First Church had revealed large gaps, especially in the care of children. Their findings led them to invite parents to include their children in the initial dinner and discussion. While the adults reviewed the congregation's grief ministry, the younger members met separately and discussed the same questions and issues with trained personnel. The result was a grief-ministry program of training and care, directed to children and adolescents as well as adults. The evening concluded with the decision to continue meeting as a grief-support group. The group affirmed the procedure adopted to introduce the concept and recommended that it be followed when other pastoral functions in the congregation were reviewed.

Following presentation of the report of the meeting to the council of the congregation, the council adopted the following procedure:

1. *Appropriate family data will be gathered and recorded, including:*
   a. wedding anniversary dates of married members;
   b. birthdays of congregants, including children;
   c. dates of deaths of members.

2. *A Grief Ministry team will be recruited and trained, and will minister under the supervision of the pastoral staff.*

Effective and compassionate support to bereaved families requires the selection and training of members to provide this ministry on behalf of the congregation. At First Church, the realization that the effort to minister to each bereaved family is beyond the reach of the clergy staff was one of the first conclusions reached by First Church's parish council. The numbers of bereaved families in their first twelve months of bereavement, and of members still grieving deaths beyond the first year, made it clear that a team of laypeople would be needed, and determined the number of people to be trained. The selection and training of a lay team is the keystone of the entire program. In congregations of up to 300 members with few deaths of congregants, the bereavement ministry will be an aspect of general pastoral care and one that any of the trained lay pastoral caregivers will be able to undertake, since it is customary to include grief ministry in lay training programs. In larger congregations with more numerous bereavements, a separate team may be trained. An initial training group of twelve people was recommended. Content of the training program should include:
   a. listening skills;
   b. understanding of the grief process, including "normal" and "complicated" grief;
   c. familiarity with planning a funeral, including a visit to a funeral home;
   d. planning and scheduling continuing pastoral care of grieving families.

3. *Following the death of a member of the congregation:*
   a. A member of the First Church pastoral-care team will be assigned to initiate the pastoral ministry relationship.
   b. A "calendar" for grief ministry during the first twelve months will be developed. It will list the family birthdays, special days as indicated (e.g., Mother's Day and Father's Day, wedding anniversary, high school graduation, or other days of special significance to the family), and the first anniversary of the member's death.
   c. At an appropriate time early in the period of mourning, a "grief inventory" may be developed with the family, to assist them to reflect on previous losses and changes the family has undergone which may be unresolved, and perhaps not even recognized as sources of grief. This process should help to identify any special needs of survivors.
   d. The ministry to the family will be reviewed with the pastoral caregiver at monthly meetings of the care team, or more often if indicated, adapting pastoral ministry to the changing needs of family members.

This outline is now applied to First Church's ministry to Mary and her family:

The Congregation's Ministry to the Gibson Family

During the six months prior to John's death, Pastor Richard Roberts had used opportunities to identify the congregation's support of grieving families as an important function of First Church's pastoral-care ministry. In sermons and education events, he had alerted the congregation to the impact of grief in members' lives. For example, he expressed his hope that whenever possible, members would attend funerals and memorial services as an expression of the congregation's care of its members. The result was apparent at John's funeral service, held at First Church. Although Mary and John were not widely known in the congregation, the sanctuary was almost filled.

Following his visit with Mary two days after John's funeral, Richard Roberts visited Mary one week later, accompanied by Jane, the lay pastor assigned to Mary's family:

Mary: Come in, Pastor. Thanks for coming.

Richard: Thanks, Mary. I understand you and Jane know one another.

Mary: Yes, we have met in the Disciples class on Sunday mornings. It's good to see you, Jane.

Jane: Thanks, Mary. How are you doing?

Mary: Oh, you know how it is. Some days I don't know if I can get through the day. Other times, there are so many things to do, I don't know where to turn.

Richard: It's hard to focus on details when grief consumes all your energy.

Mary: I guess so. I just have to pull myself together, I suppose.

Jane: I know you feel that you were just beginning to settle in when John died. You must feel a long way from your family in Flint just now.

Mary: Yes, I feel very cut off. Elizabeth flew home yesterday with the boys. Part of me is thankful for the quiet. At age 4 and 2, they are quite a handful. John, Jr. and Jimmy are back at school. So the house feels empty. Of course, I have been accustomed to have it to myself during the day, but now, I can almost hear the silence.

Richard: Jane and I have shared with each other that we didn't know John well. He had told me he had served as a deacon in Flint. I was looking forward to getting to know him, and hoped as time went on, that he would consider serving with us. We feel for you very much. You must feel that all sorts of plans have come to a grinding halt.

Mary: Yes, I haven't had much time to stop until the last few days. I was sitting here yesterday wondering how it could happen so suddenly. Last Christmas we had such big hopes for this move. Now John won't be here for Christmas this year. It will be very empty. . . . It was hard to move away from our families—they are all in the Flint area—but things had been hard up there, and when John got the job here, it seemed as if things were going right for us, for a change. It is hard to realize that everything has just fallen apart.

Richard: Mary, I guess that, in time, you would have worked through leaving your family and moving, settling into a new neighborhood, and adapting to the South with John as a part of that experience. Without him, you not only have to work through your grief at his death, but now, the move and separation from your family must add to your pain.

Mary: As I said, it still feels as if everything is whirling around, and it's all a bit unreal yet.

Jane: We cannot take the place of your own family, but we want you to feel part of our family here. You mentioned that Elizabeth flew home yesterday. Is she doing all right after John's death?

Mary: More or less. I had mixed feelings about her going. But there were some problems with Elizabeth. It was best for her to return to Flint. I really appreciate your coming round. I'm sure I will be all right. I didn't even ask you if you would like some coffee.

With the abrupt change of subject, both Richard and Jane felt it was an appropriate point at which to leave. Coffee was declined, and they left after a few minutes of small talk. A week later, Jane called Mary and arranged to visit her the following day:

Jane: Thanks for asking me to drop in. I have thought of you often. I have not had to face my husband's death, and I'm not sure where I would start. Are things beginning to come together, or is it still too soon to plan very much ahead?

Mary: I am working with John's firm and our attorney, so most of the business arrangements are under way. I keep putting off thinking about the future, I guess. It will still be there in three months time—or six months—however long it takes before one must make those sorts of decisions.

Jane: Mary, you mentioned last week that you have some mixed feelings about Elizabeth's leaving for Flint. I sensed there was some pain there for you that added to the pain of John's death.

Mary: It's a long story, Jane. Elizabeth divorced Bill three months ago, and John and I just didn't understand her. I still don't. She called one night soon after we arrived here and told us she was leaving Bill. John thought the world of Bill. They were like father and son, and John, Jr., and Jimmy thought of him as an older brother. He was a good husband and father. I still don't know

> what got into her. She wanted to move down here, and
> John was so angry with her, he wouldn't hear of it.

> **Jane:** Those memories and the hurt must add to your grief
> now, Mary. You have to work through your grief at
> John's death, and all the while, you must be grieving
> over Elizabeth's divorce.

> **Mary:** I hadn't thought of it as grief, Jane. Yes, I guess that
> makes losing John harder. I don't have him to talk things
> over with. I miss the two little ones . . . and Bill. He
> was such a help after the business in Flint went
> bankrupt. I guess I hadn't told you about that.

Mary described briefly John's dream of owning his own engineering
business, the investment of all their savings in "John's dream," and the
economic recession which had destroyed their dreams. The story was
interspersed with tears.

At one point, Mary apologized: "I haven't cried in front of anyone
since the day after John died." There was a period of silence, then Jane
continued:

> **Jane:** Mary, it isn't just grief at John's death you have to work
> through. You have shared a whole load of grief with me:
> Elizabeth's divorce, the change in John's and your
> relationship with her, the bankruptcy before that, then
> the move here. . . . John's death would have been pain
> enough—but it is weighed down with other griefs. It is
> almost as if you scarcely had time to draw breath after
> one loss when you were faced by the next. I'm not sure
> how I can help, but I want to very much.

> **Mary:** Just talking about it with you has been a help. You
> know, I hadn't thought much about it. I guess it hadn't
> occurred to me that I have grieved about leaving
> Flint—or even over losing the business. The trouble is
> that at times I still feel angry about going through our
> savings. That is where everything started to go
> wrong . . . and it hasn't let up.

Mary wept as she struggled with her feelings of hurt, buried anger,
yearning for John, and loneliness. She described how, after the
bankruptcy, John had been so depressed, she felt she couldn't tell him
she was angry with him for overcoming her reluctance to "put all their
eggs in one basket." She had been afraid that if she expressed her
anger, John would only become more depressed. And in the face of
John's guilt, she was silent.

Now she said, "The other problem, I guess, is that I'm really angry at me. I could have told John at the time that I thought it unwise to use all our savings to start the business."

Jane remained silent, as she had at other moments, sensing that during the silences, Mary was getting in touch with parts of her grief for the first time, and in those moments, needed some time to think things through. Jane's silences gave Mary the opportunity to begin to trace the web of grief in which she felt trapped. Jane's visit, followed by later visits, offered a relationship that Mary accepted and used to work through her grief—making her grief "public" was an important step toward its resolution.

It may be noted that in other circumstances, with different people, the issues might not have been raised, might not have been raised in the same way, or might not have been opened up so early in the course of bereavement. The course of grief ministry can never be fully anticipated, for it will be shaped by the personalities of caregiver and member, the "chemistry" of their relationship, the existence or absence of previous unresolved griefs, the circumstances of the death, and innumerable other factors. This account is offered not as *the* way to shape ministry; it is how Jane fashioned *her* ministry with this particular person. My purpose is to dramatize that it was helpful, and perhaps critical, to Mary's resolution of grief that she was able to recognize that her previous "griefs" still had not been resolved when John died, that they almost certainly intensified her bereavement and must be faced and dealt with on the path toward reconstituting her life. Mary is likely to achieve this goal more effectively and more speedily with the support of a friend and minister like Jane.

Development of Ministry with Children and Youth

In congregations that have failed to develop an effective grief ministry for members like Mary, it is even less likely that her two teenage sons would receive significant support. Little attention has been given in clergy education to preparing pastors and priests to identify and minister to the pastoral needs of children—particularly children in grief. Few pastors speak of offering grief care to children; some pastors, like other adults, are uncomfortable doing so. It seems that most congregations have overlooked children in grief. Individuals in the congregation—for example, junior- or senior-high counselors or church-school teachers, may be sensitive to these needs and minister to children, but few congregations have developed intentional grief-support programs that address the special needs of children.

Action should be taken at two levels: First, effective grief ministry needs to be available to children as well as adults. Second, grief-education programs to assist the congregation to recognize and respond to the needs of both adults and children should be developed. Education concerns will be discussed in chapter 5. First, we will turn to pastoral care of grieving children.

1. Responding to Preadolescent Children in Grief

Dying and death are appropriate areas to explore with children, both at home and in the congregation. Indeed, it is difficult to ignore dying and death, and the pain and anguish of grief; these concerns intrude into all our lives. Clergy, church-school teachers, and children's and youth counselors are in a unique position both to discern indications that a child is grieving and to assist children to verbalize their feelings. Remember that failure to identify and resolve fundamental aspects of grief may hinder a child's emotional ability to handle crises and grieving, and impair the ability to enter into mature relationships.

Many adults are ambivalent about discussing dying and death even with other adults; it may be especially difficult to do so with children. If you are anxious about doing so, you are not alone. But death is an inescapable part of life. We must deal with it, and so must our children. If we are to help them, we must let them know it is all right to talk about grief and about the fears that are evoked when we think or talk about dying and death.

Introduction of these topics to children may lead to various types of acting-out behavior which serves as outlets for grief. If such behaviors are substitutes for more direct expressions of grief, they may be misperceived and become the focus of irritation, rather than leading to a response to the underlying hurt and pain of loss or feared loss. On the other hand, inappropriate or changed behaviors may be indications that a child is grieving unnoticed, and may be an opportunity to address the child's needs. Careful planning should precede the introduction of both care and education programs, including training of adult caregivers and educators, and selection of materials.

Adults may feel uncomfortable if unable readily to answer all children's questions; children seem to expect parents and teachers to be all-knowing—even about death. But death, the one certainty in life, is life's greatest mystery. Dealing with death can be a lifelong process. It is appropriate to share both beliefs and doubts with children. "I don't know the answer to that one" will sometimes be the simplest and best response. Always offer to assist the child to find answers to the questions for which you do not have a ready answer. If the questions concern beliefs and practices different from one's own, it may help to tell children that people have different beliefs, that not everyone believes as we do.

Since modeling of attitudes and behaviors is a significant aspect of adult-child relationships, adults should not be afraid to let children see and feel their own grief at appropriate times. Being open with our own grief may encourage children to share their deepest fears about death. That, in turn, will help children who are facing their individual griefs to do so more openly. As caregivers become aware of how children are facing grief, they are enabled to shape their support in the most effective manner.

Children's Developmental Stages

A child who is old enough to love is old enough to grieve. However, clinical-psychology studies indicate that, depending on stage of development, children perceive such concepts as dying and death in quite different ways. Preschool children usually think of death as reversible and temporary. Since they have not yet begun to think abstractly, their world is perceived in concrete terms, a perception that may be reinforced by what they watch on TV. For example, cartoon characters magically rise up whole again—like the coyote in "Roadrunner"! Between the ages of five and nine years, most children begin to realize that death is final and that all living things die. Yet they still do not see death as personal; somehow, it won't strike them or the people they love. They may associate death with a bad or evil power which stalks people, and their fears may be expressed in concerns that parents will lose them, or not be there when they are needed. Such fears may show up in nightmares. From nine or ten years through adolescence, children begin to accept death as irreversible, that all living things die. Teenagers may become intrigued with death, or even take unnecessary risks as a sort of dare, perhaps trying to overcome their fears by bravado.

The most important caveat to these assumptions is that children do not fit into rigid categories. They develop at their own rates and have their own ways of expressing and handling feelings. Children are individually shaped by their respective experiences. Some may express curiosity about death by the age of three, while others may rarely, perhaps never, talk about death.[3] Preschool children may carry deep fears that a parent may die because that happened in a playmate's family. Apart from family deaths, children view TV reports of shootings on city streets, and some know of friends who died by suicide. They see TV pictures of children dying from starvation in Africa, or in nightly reports from Yugoslavia or other violence-ridden areas.

Responding to Violent Death

Parents and other caregivers have little choice but to address violent death when it occurs in the neighborhood or is reported on TV screens. When death is violent, caregivers should recognize that children's anxieties are sharpened by such events and anticipate both their sorrow and their need for reassurance of their safety or that of their parents. But they are also learning that life is fraught with risks, the possibility of dying and death, and the pain of anticipated separation from loved ones. They need to hear that most people act responsibly and do not go around killing or hurting each other. When death has occurred violently, children may need support and reassurance for extended periods.

More than anything else, children need honest and direct responses to their questions and concerns about dying, death, and grief. Their greatest need is our sympathetic and nonjudgmental response. They will be quick to notice whether we are uncomfortable with their comments or questions. If so, honesty may be our most important response.

Talking to the Young Child

Following the enthusiastic nationwide response of community caregivers to the SCI series, "Working Through Your Grief," the corporation produced a second video presentation, "A Child's View of Grief." In an accompanying booklet, Alan Wolfelt notes that, "handled with warmth and understanding, a child's early experiences of death can be opportunities to learn about life and living as well as death and dying."[4] He suggests that children are the "forgotten mourners." Because adults often are unable to help children address grief openly, children may not have the opportunity to express their feelings at all, and may develop distorted attitudes concerning death, dying, and funerals. These attitudes may remain with them for the rest of their lives.

Children need answers to their questions and responses that are addressed forthrightly to the child at his or her level of comprehension. Children learn through repetition, so caregivers may stimulate the same questions again and again, and offer the same answer. Patience is needed when children seem to have forgotten the answer to a question asked a number of times; they may be asking for further clarification and sharing of ideas, or indicating that concern and anxiety about death are deeper than an adult at first perceived. It may take time for a child to understand all the nuances of one's answers. Although six-year-old Judith knows that her Uncle Ed died, she may want to know why her aunt is crying. A response may be: "Aunt Susan is crying because she is sad that Uncle Ed has died. She misses him very much. We all feel sad when someone we care about dies."

One of the most disconcerting aspects of children's comments and questions is that they are asked from the child's perspective and curiosity. Questions may seem shockingly insensitive to adults, but they may be the child's way of seeking further knowledge or reassurance. For example, "When will you die?" may catch an adult off-balance. Adults should expect the unexpected! Children may express themselves in ways for which adults are unprepared. One grandmother was sitting with her family, awaiting the beginning of her husband's funeral service. Her four-year-old grandson edged down the row of adults and took his place beside her. Noticing the tears on her cheeks, he patted her knee gently and said, "Don't be sad, Grandma. We'll get you another old man!"

Children's anxieties about dying and death and, particularly, the deaths of family members or classmates, are shaped by the respective family settings in which they are growing up. Adults should anticipate children's anxieties that parents might die and leave them helpless and alone. Being cared for is not a worry just for preschoolers or nine-year-olds. Even teenagers may be well aware that they are not yet old enough to take responsibility for themselves; and in any case, they cannot bear to think of being parted from their parents. A twenty-six-year-old son said to his father, "I'm not ready to go it alone just yet! Take care of yourself!" In the event of terminal illness or death in his or her family, a child may carry these concerns to day school or church school. For example, one student may be preoccupied and inattentive, while another may act out anxiety in the classroom. A third may verbalize anxieties to adults, perhaps indicating a strong need for reassurance.

Responding to Children's Misperceptions

Children may acquire many misperceptions about death from other children or from careless adults.

a. Young children may confuse death with sleep, because someone was heard to say that "Nana went to sleep." *But Nana went to sleep and was buried! What about me?*

b. Trying to spare a grandchild's anxiety, her grandmother told the child that Uncle Ed had "gone away." *But Uncle Ed went away and hasn't come back, and Aunt Susan is crying all the time.*

c. Children may be confused about illness and hospitalization, unless reality is tempered with reassurance. Preschoolers cannot differentiate between minor and terminal illnesses. Some minor ailments may leave them with underlying fears. When talking with a child about someone who died after becoming sick and going to the hospital, it might be helpful to explain that only a very serious illness may cause death, and that although we all get sick at times, we usually get better again. When a child informs you that a family member is in the hospital, listen for indications that the child is dealing with underlying fears of loss and separation, and, perhaps, death.

d. Another generalization we unthinkingly may make relates to death in old age. Saying, "Only old people die," or "Nana died because she was old," can lead to distrust, when a child learns that young people can die too. It might be better to say, "Nana lived a long time before she died. Most people live a long time, but some don't. I expect you and I will."[5]

One of the most important messages children can hear is that, no matter what happens, there are plans for their well-being and security. Some parents will assist children to accept such terrifying outcomes as the death of a parent by discussing with their children the plans parents have made if this eventuality should occur. In any event, it is difficult, if not impossible, to improve on truth-telling with children. Remember, also, that the event of a death may rekindle curiosity—or fear—in a child who has already experienced the death of a family member. The earlier death may have occurred years before, but the feelings of insecurity or doubt may "recycle" with each new experience of bereavement in the child's life.

Some Children's Reactions to a Death in the Family

Some people may experience guilt when a loved one dies. Young children in particular have difficulty understanding cause-and-effect relationships, and may think that in some way they caused the death: Maybe their angry thoughts or words provoked the death. Or they may see death as a punishment: "Mom died and left me because I was bad." Children may be helped to cope with guilt by reassuring them that they always have been loved and still are. It may also help to explain the circumstances of the death. *The notion that death is a form of punishment should never be reinforced.*

The death of a family member may arouse feelings of anger in both adults and children. Mourners may feel angry with the person who died for causing so much pain and sorrow, or for leaving them alone to cope with life. Some people may feel angry at the doctors and nurses who could not save the loved one, while others may feel angry at themselves for being unable to prevent the death, or for not doing enough while the person was dying. Children may express their angry thoughts openly, especially when someone on whom they depended for love and care has died. It is difficult enough to hear anger directed toward the dead, and even more so when it is expressed for what appear to be selfish concerns (see also chapter 6).

But since anger may accompany grief, parents who are struggling with their own grief may find that they have to deal with their own anger at the very same time they are called upon to assist their children to struggle with anger. Their relationships are likely to be tested much more if children act out anger within the family, toward neighbors, or at school. Caregivers should recognize that these are not unusual aspects of response to grief. Parents may be helped with reassurance that the occurrence of acting-out behavior offers them an opportunity to explore with their children the feelings they are experiencing and to reaffirm their love for their family, learning, as they do so, to avoid scolding a child whose anger has spilled over. Children may act out anger in a variety of ways—in overt anger, becoming withdrawn and depressed, or developing physical symptoms. Parents and caregivers should be alert for these signs. If noted in congregational settings, they may be brought to parents' attention in the context of the congregation's pastoral ministry to the family.

School Staff Response to the Death of a Child or Teacher

When Anne, a child in St. John's Sunday morning church school, died, parish staff members realized that in addition to their ministry to their grieving family, they needed to think through how to care for the members of Anne's class. Parents of the children were informed of Anne's death and invited to attend the funeral with their children. Subsequent to the funeral, the parish pastoral-care committee proposed, as part of the congregation's grief care and education program, that parents be invited to assist in developing a parish curriculum to provide educational materials for each age group, from kindergarten to the oldest members (see chapter 6).

The parents endorsed the following guidelines which the church school staff had proposed, in response to the death of a child or an adult with whom children have been closely associated.

a. Children may be invited to remember a child's (or adult's) achievements and special contributions. Reliving memories is an important aspect of mourning.

b. Enabling children to talk about the death of a friend is a step toward identifying and addressing any fears and anxieties children may have about death.

c. Parents should anticipate the possibility of children wishing to attend a church funeral. The decision to do so was recognized as a parental responsibility.

d. In addition to providing for response to a death in classroom activities, children may be encouraged to bring individual concerns to teachers. Some children may be unable to address these matters in open class discussions.

e. Church-school classes may visit a mortuary so that children may become familiar with funeral procedures.

The Teacher's Relationship with Parents

The extent to which teachers will feel free to address these issues with children in church-school classes will depend upon close relationships with each child's parents. If, for example, a teacher becomes concerned with a child's behavior following a death in his or her family, it is appropriate to consult with the parent(s). First, a phone call or note, or visit to the home, is an opportunity to express sympathy for the family. This will be appreciated and will strengthen the teacher's general relationship with parents. Second, teachers may ask whether there are any particular concerns with which they should be familiar.

Remember: Children Also Mourn

Mourning is the recognition of a deeply felt loss, and it is a process we all must work through before we can pick up the pieces and go on living fully and normally again. Mourning heals. By being open to our own sorrows and tears, we show our children that it is all right to feel sad and to cry. Expressions of grief should never be equated with weakness. Boys as well as girls should be allowed to cry and express their feelings if and when they need to. A child may show little immediate grief and may seem unaffected by the loss. Some mental-health experts believe that children are not mature enough to work through a deeply felt loss unaided, and the process may be delayed until adolescence. Consequently, they say, children may express their sadness on and off over a long period of time, and often at unexpected moments. Adults may find it painful to have old wounds probed again and again. But children need patience, understanding, and support to complete their "grief work."

2. Adolescents' Grief Needs

Behaviors experienced frequently in young children may continue into adolescence. For example, Tommy and Richard, age eight and fourteen, were informed by their parents that their grandfather, to whom they were very close, had died. Ten minutes later, to their parents' surprise and concern, they were throwing baskets in the driveway. Tommy and Richard were grieving, but neither had any pattern that would inform them as to their appropriate response. It was not simply that they were unsure how children were expected to respond—they just did not know what to do with all the feelings they were experiencing.

But one of the bonds that had tied them to their grandfather was their shared pleasure in throwing basketballs in the driveway. Their spontaneous reaction was to do what they had most enjoyed doing with him—that was where they felt closest to him, and it seemed the place to be to remember him. Children often manifest behaviors when bereaved that are unaccountable to adults. They should not be *expected* to match the mourning behaviors of adults, for they do not possess the experiences that prepare adults to face grief. And even adults do not always respond to grief in mature ways!

The grief work for adolescents is more complex than for adults, because they are struggling through grief at a time when other fundamental and disturbing life changes are being worked through. Adolescence is usually characterized by concern with issues of independence, peer acceptance, and self-esteem. This may complicate the tasks of working through grief for teenagers, since such concerns may be accompanied by anxieties about physical development, appearance, and even deportment. Teenagers may be concerned about their relationships with peers, or a particular peer. The break-up of a first (or any) romance may be felt as a catastrophic loss and grieved deeply. Responses may be more extreme, either more volatile or more depressed, since working through the normal developmental stages makes it harder to work through grief, "to mourn in constructive, healthy ways."[6]

Wolfelt suggests some specific indicators that a teenager is becoming immobilized by grief: Symptoms may include chronic depression, sleep disturbances, restlessness, low self-esteem, disinterest in academic achievement, deterioration in personal relationships with family members and friends, difficulty in forming significant relationships, and denial of grief characterized by efforts toward hypermaturity. Acting-out behaviors may include use of drugs or alcohol, rage, inappropriate risk-taking, or sexual behavior.[7]

Adults' expectations that teenagers somehow must begin to take adult roles is one of the most onerous burdens that adults may place upon adolescents. A fourteen-year-old boy talks about this: "All the male relatives said that you have to be strong, that you should take care of your mother, and do everything that your father did. That's stupid. You don't know . . . you don't have half of the knowledge he had. There's no sense in trying to take care of family. I'm only fourteen . . . so how can I?"[8]

Mourning is a process, not an event, for children and adolescents as well as for adults. The congregation can do much to support parents and to provide grief ministry to young people. These efforts should be undertaken through carefully designed and supervised grief-support programs oriented to the special needs of children and youth.

The Caregiver's Own Griefs

Grief is more widespread and intrusive in our daily lives than most people realize, and none of us can escape its reach. Grief ministry is possible at the most profound depths only when caregivers are ready to risk being touched by the anguish of the bereaved people for whom they are caring. Only when that anguish has been plumbed to its often bitter depths can pastoral ministry to people in grief be assured of integrity. For example, children's needs to explore bereavement may come just at a time when caregivers are most vulnerable to their own painful memories and as yet unresolved griefs. Parents may be so preoccupied with their own griefs that they are less aware of their children's needs. An alert teacher or lay grief minister may notice that a child appears to be struggling with his or her grief and inquire if the parent is aware of the situation.

It is difficult to anticipate such moments, but they are less difficult to face if one is aware of the possibility that they may occur. In any event, wise adults ensure that they have their own avenues through which to address such personal needs as grief and bereavement. Most of us, as individuals, need resources to help us face and work through grief. If we use them well, we will be better able to serve as resources to other people.

One of the avenues through which the grief needs of adults and children can be addressed is the provision of grief-support groups. This ministry is developed in chapter 5.

CHAPTER 5

Grief Support:
A Continuing Ministry

Tell them, that, to ease them of their griefs,
Their fears of hostile strokes, their aches, losses,
Their pangs of love, with other incident throes
That nature's fragile vessel doth sustain
In life's uncertain voyage,
I will some kindness do them.

TIMON OF ATHENS V.i.203

The Duration of Mourning

The needs of bereaved families or individuals are usually acute at identifiable times during the period of mourning, and, as indicated, may extend throughout the first year and beyond. Even if the intensity of grief begins to wane, there are days—and nights—when sadness and loneliness cause fresh, intense pain. It is at those times that people in grief are most in need of comfort and support. The congregation would seem to be one oasis from which the mourner would be refreshed. When its members are unaware of the grieving person's needs, and clergy are overwhelmed by competing demands and needs, however, bereaved families often are overlooked, and feel forgotten.

If the staff and members of First Church had overlooked the needs of Mary and her sons during her first year of grief, it is even less likely that they would receive support in subsequent years. Yet bereavement needs do not simply fade away with the end of the initial period of mourning, regardless of whether that extends for just a few months, or throughout the first year. This became very evident during an evening worship in a large congregation.

The Grief Ministry session of the Equipping Laypeople for Ministry (ELM) workshop was almost over. We had been reflecting on the needs of grieving families during their first twelve months of bereavement when the conversation was interrupted by Bob: "I suppose you all remember that today is the third anniversary of Judy's death." There was a long silence. The fifteen members sitting around the table looked helplessly at one another and at Bob. None of them had remembered, and they felt guilty. Bob was a retired former minister of the congregation, and Judy, his wife, had been a beloved member and friend of each member of the group. But none of them had remembered that this was the third anniversary of Judy's death.

To be fair to the group, this failure to remember is not surprising. When Judy died, their normal routines and lives had not been interrupted and changed as Bob's had been. And three years later, few individuals could be expected to remember the date's significance. But Bob expected the *congregation* to remember. And therein lay his pain: Everyone had forgotten. The following story emerged.

Bob's responsibility as pastor emeritus included two hours morning and afternoon when he visited members in their homes. That morning, he had arrived at the church offices at 9:30, wandered into the work areas and pastors' offices and greeted his colleagues, then left for his morning visits. He spent lunchtime with the church staff, and at 2:00, left to make his afternoon calls. Instead of returning home at 4:00, he came back to the church and again wandered around greeting people. It began to dawn on us as we listened to Bob's story that he had been waiting all day for someone at the church to remember and share his grief! Bob experienced the failure to remember as a lack of care that deepened his pain.

I heard stories like Bob's in most cities I visited. Some responsibility surely rests on the grieving person to communicate his or her need, but for a variety of reasons, many people seem unable to initiate a request for remembering and grief care. In any event, regardless of an individual's ability or readiness to seek support, the congregation has not only the opportunity but the responsibility to extend continuing care to its members in grief, and that care is often needed year after year.

Lindemann, addressing his psychiatric peers, has, in fact, provided directions for all of us who care for bereaved people. He stated that the primary task of the caregiver is "that of sharing the [mourner's] grief work, namely, his efforts at extricating himself from the bondage to the deceased and finding new patterns of rewarding interaction."[1] Lindemann recognized that grieving people often cannot accomplish the tasks of grieving unaided, and the caregiver's support may be decisive in completing this process.

Lindemann reminded caregivers that it is important to note both overreaction and underreaction to grief, "because delayed responses may occur at unpredictable moments and the dangerous distortions of the grief reaction, not conspicuous at first, be quite destructive later and these may be prevented."[2] While Lindemann was addressing psychotherapists, and acute grief reactions may indicate the need to refer the sufferer for medical care, most bereaved people work through their grief without becoming so disabled. The support of trained lay caregivers may be all that is needed to assist a mourner to work through grief. But such support usually is not available unless planned and supervised.

Lindemann stressed accessibility to care from the mourner's religious community as an important source of help to the bereaved. Noting that "religious agencies" have led in dealing with the bereaved, he suggested that they provide comfort by giving the backing of dogma to the mourner's wish for continued interaction with the deceased, use rituals that maintain his or her interaction with others, and may counteract morbid guilt feelings by divine grace and by promising an opportunity for "making up" to the deceased at the time of later reunion.

Yet he warns that although these measures may assist mourners, "comfort alone does not provide adequate assistance in the bereaved person's grief work"; the mourner still must bear the pain of bereavement, review relationships with the deceased, and be aware of the alterations in his or her own modes of emotional interaction. Fear of irrational responses, of accepting the turmoil of feelings that are part of grief, especially the overflow of hostility, must be worked through. Through the expression of sorrow and sense of loss, the mourner can find an acceptable formulation of future relationships with the deceased. Lindemann recognized that not all bereaved people need psychotherapeutic help and that clergy and other caregivers may assist mourners to work through the more normal grief reactions, referring people with "more ominous pictures" for psychiatric help.[3]

Parkes also affirmed the role of clergy in helping bereaved people to work through grief. His concern was that few physicians—or clergy—receive formal training for such ministry. That situation is still unchanged. While medical schools and seminaries provide lectures on "Death and Dying," patients or families may experience insensitivity to their grieving from their physicians, and congregants may fail to receive adequate or effective care for them and their families during their bereavement. Clergy continuing-education seminars on dying, death, and grief are usually well attended. But the fact that, in 97 percent of a representative national sample of congregations, the basic elements of grief management are missing, indicates the need for more than educational events that merely analyze "the grief process."

Writing thirty years after Lindemann, Parkes had the advantage of the research that his predecessor had inspired. He pointed to the emergence of "bereavement counseling" in his chapter "Helping the Bereaved," and suggested management strategies that focus on predeath, or anticipatory grief, needs; the immediate post-death period; and long-term grief care.[4] Most clergy provide for their congregants' needs prior to the death of ill family members and in the immediate post-death period, by visitation with the family prior to the funeral, the conduct of the funeral, and in the ensuing ten days to two weeks. Members of congregations usually support their grieving families with comforting visits, prepared meals, phone calls, and flowers. Yet most grieving families express a sense of being overlooked as their mourning extends throughout the first year and beyond, and the lives of other congregants return to normal. Parkes notes that mourners often speak positively about the help they received at the time of the funeral. Many remember who was present, though fewer seem to place importance on, or even remember, what was said.

Parkes emphasized the importance of the transition from early to later grief work. In the early period, family and friends rally round the bereaved and relieve them of some of their roles and obligations. Later, when the mourner faces the task of establishing his or her own autonomy, support is often still needed, both to help the mourner to grieve and then to move beyond mourning, "to give up his withdrawal from life and to start building a new identity."[5]

Congregations must now direct their attention to the equipment of lay caregivers to provide this support. With an adequate understanding of the grief process and the development of basic listening skills, sensitive laypeople who have resolved their own griefs sufficiently may provide effective grief support to others. They can develop a ministry that includes the readiness not only to support people in mourning, but to challenge them to recognize and affirm the turning points as they are reached. They will need to be alert to indicators that a bereaved person is not moving toward resolution and make appropriate referrals to the congregation's pastoral staff.

For example, Parkes suggested, close observation may indicate that while grief is expected and permitted, mourning has gone on long enough; it may take an outsider to point out that the duty to the dead has been met and that "the mourner can be permitted to let up a little." Of course, in the absence of such continuing care, it is likely that the bereaved person will get little encouragement to mourn at any time. "But when grief has broken through it may take a special circumstance to get the mourner out of a state of habitual mourning."[6] Parkes suggests that while it is important for the bereaved person to grieve, it is just as important to move beyond mourning and begin the task of building a new identity, separate from the deceased.

Among the "turning points" that bereaved people may be assisted to identify and pursue with the help of caregivers are decisions to rearrange furniture, take vacations, enroll in educational programs, or implement plans that were deferred by marriage or family responsibilities. The first anniversary of the death is usually an important turning point. Parkes cites a widow who went on a vacation eleven months after her husband's death stating, "For the first time I have the feeling that I can make it. The anniversary itself was painful, but within three weeks she went to a dance for the first time."

Parkes' review of this case is revealing: "It was the second new year after her husband's death, however, that constituted the decisive turning point. Here she met, at a party, a fellow 'orphan of the storm' and henceforth she saw him regularly. A year later she became formally engaged, but only on the eve of her second wedding did she start to refer, in her diary, to her first husband in the past tense."[7]

It is because full realization comes in steps, as Parkes affirms, that other people are involved in these steps.[8] Without the support of others it is hard to give up habits of withdrawal and mourning. In the absence of congregational support programs, secular groups have sprung up in many communities to fill the gap, or provide group activities to people who do not have relationships with congregations.

Worden places the same emphases in *Grief Counseling and Grief Therapy*. Although he does not focus on long-term grief support as narrowly as does Parkes, Worden's insights highlight each section of his book. For example, he reminds us that social factors can play an extremely important part in the development of complicated grief reactions and, consequently, in their alleviation: "Grief is really a social process and is best dealt with in a social setting in which people can support and reinforce each other in their reactions to the loss."[9] He states that the *absence* of a social support network may result in prolonged grief work. Geographic factors shape the lives of many people, restricting access to a significant support network to phone calls and letters.

But a support network may be missing because of *social isolation*. Worden cites Parkes' 1972 London study which explored the relationship between anger and social isolation.[10] A widow who received much support from her friends immediately following her husband's death was extremely angry six months later because no one was approaching her or calling her. Her anger probably pushed people away, but the incident emphasizes the need for caregivers to initiate contact with bereaved people with offers of support. Although directed to grief therapists, Worden's "clues" to unresolved grief reactions will certainly inform clergy, and may be used in training lay caregivers for ministry in the congregation.

Davidson outlines his concept of the process of mourning in a book addressed to the mourner, which caregivers, particularly lay pastoral ministers, will find a valuable resource.[11] The book is a longitudinal study of 1200 adult mourners and reports their progress toward grief resolution. Davidson identifies common misunderstandings concerning mourning: that it "normally" lasts up to two weeks; that staying busy is the best way to handle grief; that grief is a private matter; that men are not as affected as women; and that mourners should forget the deceased and "go on."[12]

Like Worden, Davidson addresses the usefulness of identifying grief using "disease" categories. He uses examples from the lives of his research subjects to sketch the course of mourning during the first twelve months, noting that one of the most anxious questions mourners ask is, "When will I get over my grief?" He uses the categories of orientation/disorientation and reorganization to delineate the grief process: "Mourning is a universal experience that is intensely disorienting and lonely, yet it is widely misunderstood by both laity and the trained professionals. . . . Mourning is a complex set of emotions, which, if allowed to function appropriately, can help in the reorientation process."[13]

He concludes that there are five attributes that seem to determine the degree to which mourners can work through their grief—namely, the extent to which they are in touch with and act to meet "basic survival" needs; their level of self-esteem; their ability to continue to relate to others; their readiness and ability to improve coping skills; and their openness to "improved understanding of how people function, feel, and take meaning from life."[14]

Special Grief Needs Evoked by Trauma or Crisis

Regardless of the circumstances of the loss, the mourner experiences the pain of grief, with all the feelings it evokes, as uniquely his or her own. "No one else can understand what it feels like to me," Mary told her lay pastor, Jane. It is not possible to measure one person's pain against another's. Each *is* unique—as unique as a fingerprint! Yet there are some losses in which the intensity of grief appears to be sharpened by the circumstances and calls for special sensitivity on the part of caregivers.

This sense of deepened tragedy is typified by the story of a small community from which an eleven-year-old boy was abducted while riding home on his bicycle with his brother and a friend. No trace of the boy was found. A mother whose son had died as the result of illness responded that she thought her son's death was the worst pain a mother could know—until she read about this crime. There are unique instances of grief that require special responses from caregivers.

Murder. Survivors whose loved one was murdered often experience more intense feelings of rage and helplessness than those that characterize other grief experiences. Police investigations or the thought that the murderer may go unpunished frequently complicate their grief. If the accused murderer is arrested and jailed, the seemingly endless processes of the legal system may result in trial proceedings that extend over years, often requiring repeated appearances at preliminary hearings, the trial, and appeals. Survivors speak of being trapped within this "injustice system," their freedom to pick up the pieces of their lives squandered by forces beyond their control. A woman whose twenty-one-year-old son was murdered stated, "I would give anything to have my boy back. But that's not possible. The only thing left to me is to make sure his killer stays in jail."

When death is violent, the usual remembrance days (see Figure 15 above) are, if possible, even more painful. The anguish due to the cause of death may be relived at each step in the legal process, anger that seems to have no end if rekindled, and many seem unable to separate emotionally from the deceased.

Suicide. Death by suicide of a family member or close friend similarly is often accompanied by a profound sense of loss of control. Edwin Sneidman proposes that "the person who commits suicide puts his psychological skeletons in the survivors' emotional closet—he sentences the survivors to deal with many negative feelings, and, more, to become obsessed with thoughts regarding their own actual or possible role in having precipitated the suicidal act or having failed to abort it. It can be a heavy load."[15]

Survivors' burdens that complicate the work of mourning may include feelings of anger, shame, guilt, and stigma; fractured family relationships; and recurring painful memories. Worden tells of a widow who paced through her house for six months after her husband's suicide, shouting, "Damn it, if you hadn't killed yourself I would kill you for what you are putting me through."[16]

Shame and guilt may lead to self-punishing behavior, or survivors may feel a deepened sense of rejection.[17] In some instances, children may fear to approach the age at which a parent committed suicide, because of their own self-destructive thoughts. In this, as in other areas of acute grief, pastors supervising lay care teams may assist caregivers to understand the special needs of survivors by utilizing personnel from community support groups for continuing education sessions.

The Death of a Child. Many authors have addressed the special needs of parents whose children have died. Parents who have struggled with this painful grief remind us that detachment from a child feels more tragic and is often more prolonged than other types of separation. Mothers and, in many instances, fathers, begin to bond with the anticipated baby long before birth. Beverly Raphael notes that "when the baby's quickening and later first movements are clearly felt, the fantasy relationship with this fantasy child intensifies. The naming of the baby, the rehearsal for parenting, the fantasies shared with the father, the reality of the child, come to the fore."[18] Miscarriage for both parents may thus result in profound grief.

Bonding strengthens with each day, through the birth and throughout childhood, varying in form and intensity as the child grows toward adult maturity. It undergoes a substantial change when the child leaves the home as a young adult.[19] This maturation process, with its accompanying losses and changes, is anticipated by most parents, who weather the changes as part of the normal joys and pains of parenthood. A child's death shatters this expected outcome of parenthood. One of the cries heard constantly from parents whose adult children have died as the result of AIDS is that "this should not have happened—he (or she) should be burying me, not the other way around." But whereas the death of an adult child is sorely felt, the death of a dependent child seems even more unspeakable. The bonds are still being forged when they are shattered by death.

Raphael notes that systematic studies of outcomes for bereavements at the childhood stage are few. She cites a study of parents of children who drowned, which found that families showed sleep disorders, nightmares, anxiety states, and increased drinking, sometimes extending over many years:

> Nineteen percent of these parents received specialist psychiatric treatment following the drowning, whereas none had done so before. Overprotection of remaining children was common, and the siblings of one-third of the cases were significantly affected with sleep disorders and feelings of guilt. . . . Clinical experience suggests that depression is a frequent symptom, often complicating a severe chronic grief reaction.[20]

The pain experienced with the child's death and the consequent disruptive impact upon family relationships may require a more compassionate response to grieving parents than many perceive was provided when their children died. Raphael notes that interpersonal relationships may suffer both at the time of the crisis and subsequently: "Strain on marital relationships (30 percent of the subjects in the Cornwell group's study [see note 21] may extend to frank marital breakdown. Many workers suggest that these problems are most likely in relationships that have already shown difficulties prior to the loss (Lowman 1979). Marital and sexual problems are described frequently in the literature."[21]

While Raphael's references are to the impact of Sudden Infant Death Syndrome (SIDS), regardless of the circumstances of a child's death, disruption of parental relationships occurs in over 50 percent of cases. Worden cites a Stanford University study that found 70 percent of the parents whose children died of leukemia were divorced within the subsequent two-year period.[22]

When death is sudden—for example, drowning, burns, or auto accident—death is not only perceived as untimely, but is more likely to be accompanied by feelings of guilt, whether appropriate or inappropriate, than if death resulted from illness. It is also more likely to evoke remorse which may linger for prolonged periods. Thus, the person responsible for the child may regret a lack of close supervision that permitted the child to wander into the swimming pool or onto the street.

These tragedies are also often accompanied by blame directed toward the person deemed to be responsible for the accident. Caregivers listening to the recounting of the details may be expected to identify with the feelings expressed by the grieving parent. It takes a special sensitivity to listen to the anguish of each party without joining in the apportionment of blame. The tragedy and its grief may be prolonged if a family witnessed the accident.

Raphael recounts how a mother's lapse of attention permitted her four-year-old to wander onto the street. When she heard a loud crash, she ran to the front door and saw neighbors gathering around her daughter's still body: "Vividly etched in her memory, replayed in slow motion are the details of the scene as she passed through her front door and out onto the street. . . . This replayed constantly, in repetitive cognitions, with periods of repression over the two years following the death." As the months wore on, helplessness, dread, and panic which were felt at that moment became intertwined with rage against the driver and God. "She had not mourned but had become fixed in time and place, neither having her child nor relinquishing her."[23]

Anger may be directed toward any person, either because it is appropriate or in an effort to avoid confronting the sense of responsibility the grieving person feels. It may be felt and expressed toward the driver of a vehicle involved in an accident, whether that is the spouse or another driver. In the case where a driver is charged with driving while intoxicated, this anger later may be channeled appropriately into such organizations as Mothers Against Drunk Driving. The decision to set aside the tempting liturgy of the "if onlys" and confront the full intensity of the loss is one of the most difficult tasks faced by surviving family members, especially the parents.

Sudden Infant Death Syndrome (SIDS). While noting that each family experiences the death of a child—or other family member—as a grief more intense than that of another person or family, SIDS hold special fears and anguish for parents. It accounts for more than eight thousand deaths per year in the United States.[24] Despite ten years of intensive investigation, the nature of SIDS and its cause(s) remain a mystery. Parents may settle their baby, which typically has been quite well, in their normal way, only to find the child dead during the night or in the morning. Death is usually "silent," with no sign to alarm parents.

The seeming futility of the parenting roles, the unexpectedness of the tragedy, and the shock of finding the apparently healthy baby dead, coalesce into an intensity of grief which many parents find themselves unable to bear. It is complicated by feelings of self-blame—in the early investigative period, police and pathology investigators often accused the parent(s) of causing the baby's death. While law-enforcement staff are now trained to recognize the special case of infant death which SIDS represents, parents can scarcely avoid feelings of guilt that they did not recognize symptoms or provide sufficient care for their baby. Family members may exacerbate such feelings by stressing the ineptitude of parents.

As with families of murder and suicide victims, it is likely that family members grieving the deaths of children will need extended support from caregivers. Preexisting family dysfunction may be acted out, and depressed states are common. Each represents a special need of survivors that may be met by lay caregivers, enhanced by specialized training and supervision from pastors and other professionals in the congregation.

Remember that while the primary function of grief ministry is the loving care and support of the survivors, this ministry also creates a learning opportunity for members of the care team. Special training events focusing on each area of family need may be arranged in consultation with community support groups related to specific needs. For example, The Compassionate Friends, a national program with local chapters, addresses the needs of parents whose children have died. A growing number of local groups, some, like Theos, with national affiliation, provide programs for widowed people. Congregations may exercise a significant ministry by sponsoring and providing facilities for such groups. But they also have another option—namely, developing a "grief-support group" for their own members.

Planning a Grief-support Group

The outline presented in chapter 4 suggested one way a grief-support program may be initiated in the congregation. A personal invitation to members of bereaved families to assist in the development of a comprehensive program emphasizes their unique place in the congregation and the opportunity it affords them to contribute to the formation of the congregation's grief ministry. Members who participate in the exploratory session may take advantage of the opportunity to continue as a grief-support group.

Grief groups, like other types of interaction groups, may take a variety of forms, depending upon the needs of individuals and the availability of group leaders. Decisions to be made include the frequency of meetings, the closed or open structure of the group, and whether the group is organized for a fixed term or has a continuing existence.

Frequency. Group facilitators may either negotiate frequency of meetings with group members, or create a structure about which members are informed as they join the group. Most community-based grief-support groups meet monthly. Congregationally based groups may meet weekly, biweekly, or monthly.

Term. Support groups may have a fixed termination point or may be open-ended, with participants free to join or leave the group at any point. Fixed-term groups, for example, of six- or eight-week sessions, may be offered at intervals throughout the year. Both structures are found to be effective. In the first instance, the flexibility of the design encourages people to benefit from the support of the group as long as they deem it helpful. They may also be encouraged to remain in the group after their immediate needs are met, so that they may contribute to care of newly arrived members. Some people may find the open-ended nature of the group less threatening than a fixed-term group. Other people may welcome the opportunity to commit to a specific term.

Format. Sessions usually begin with an invitation from the group facilitator to participants to introduce themselves and state briefly the name and cause of death of the family member or friend who died. It is wise, however, to assure members that they are free to say as much or as little as they choose about why they are present, who has died, the circumstances of the death, and when the death occurred. If new members are being welcomed, the facilitator may remind the group of any guidelines that the members have adopted. The form and content most generally followed is a nonstructured session in which, after introductions, members are free to share their personal experiences of grief and their efforts toward resolution.

At the discretion of the facilitator, sharing of individual experiences may be complemented by brief educational segments. These may be important additions, but should not detract from the main purpose of the session—namely, the sharing of individual stories. In one of my earliest groups, I set a pattern with a brief educational presentation at the start of each session, but after a few sessions, I concluded that this tended to stifle conversation. When we reverted to an unstructured format, members' contributions were more spontaneous, and participation was consistently more widespread. Didactic content may be kept to a minimum to avoid the risk of growing dependence on the group leaders' management of the sessions, and be introduced in response to a particular group or individual need.

Selection of Group Facilitators.[25] Group leaders ideally will have some professional background and skill in group management. To this end, congregants with social work or counseling skills may be recruited as co-leaders. It is recommended that groups be led by two co-leaders. Co-leadership provides ongoing supervision, accountability, support, and continuing education for both leaders. Co-leaders may complement each other's contributions, and the occasional absence of one leader does not compromise the maintenance of the group. It is important that the facilitators have completed their own grief work, or be dealing with it in another setting, so that the group process is not thwarted by the needs of the leaders. Facilitators should have access to their own support system and, ideally, to peer supervision. For example, leaders of community grief-support groups may meet regularly for supervision and continuing education.

The facilitators are responsible for group development and maintenance, and the development of care and trust within the group. This can be achieved by modeling a listening style and by assisting participants to clarify and understand one another's feelings and needs. Group leaders are also responsible for maintaining group structures, and agreed guidelines for group sessions.

Leaders should recognize their own limits and be ready to refer participants to a psychotherapist or counselor when indicated. Instances in which this is indicated may best be identified by ensuring competent supervision for the group's leaders. The selection of group facilitators may be determined by the availability (or inaccessibility) of leaders with training and experience in group leadership. However, while group management may be strengthened when leaders are professionally trained, many grief-support groups are led effectively by laypeople whose principal gifts are their openness, warmth, and empathy, and their effective resolution of their own bereavement. Many chapters of The Compassionate Friends are led by sensitive and caring people whose experience as bereaved parents and openness to the needs of other grieving parents have equipped them for their roles.

Establishing Guidelines. Specific guidelines that will shape the group's life may be offered. It is wise to begin and end meetings at the agreed times, not only because it is more orderly, but because people in grief may find it difficult to reestablish structures in their lives. This framework offers them a model they may then follow. Second, it is important to anticipate a variety of possible situations that may inhibit group interaction. For example, one person's need to monopolize the group's attention, or another's introduction of material that distracts from the group's purpose, requires sensitivity on the part of the group leader. Thus, members may be free to express how their personal faith helps in working through their own griefs, but not to infer that others should agree with and adopt that design. Group members may be invited during the first session to think about and bring to the next session additional proposals for the conduct of group meetings.

If the group has a fixed-term format—for example, eight sessions—it is important to decide at the outset whether people may be admitted to sessions, once these have begun. An alternative may be to restrict entry after the second session. One asset of the open-ended group is its facility to accept new members at any point. Some groups use an informal contracting process as an aspect of group building. For example, the decision to admit new members once the group is formed may be made by participants in the first session. It may also be resolved that members are committed to attend all sessions, except by prior agreement with the co-leaders, or to leave the group only after other members have been informed of the member's intention to terminate.

Such formal guidelines may be dismissed as overly restrictive on members' freedom to assess their needs and determine how best to meet them. Less formally structured groups may be more appropriate in some settings, and experience certainly suggests that they may be as beneficial to members as more-structured group procedures.

Grief Topics. It may be helpful to suggest to the group members a range of topics they may wish to address—for example, the events associated with the death; recollections of the course of a fatal illness; memories of the loved one; how the survivor is coping (or not coping) with grief; relationships with other family members from the perspective of the grieving person; how to discuss death with children; specific issues that address decisions that must be made following a death; the wisdom of selling a family residence; disposing of clothes and other memorabilia.[26]

Newcomers to grief-support ministries may be confronted with the decision about whether to open group sessions to congregants whose source of grief is a loss, or change, other than bereavement. Grief resulting from divorce is the most likely matter that may be raised. Most grief-group facilitators agree that while aspects of the grief process may be common to a variety of sources of grief, it is best to provide support groups that are exclusive either to bereavement or divorce. Mixing the two may be helpful neither to bereaved people nor to the newly divorced.

A congregation too small or with too few resources to provide and maintain both ministries may work with neighboring congregations to create a joint program that serves both needs for members of the congregations. Alternatively, a congregation may assist in the formation of a grief-support program open to the community. That such an initiative would be welcomed is witnessed by a small widows' support group formed in a small North Texas rural community.

During discussion in a seminar in the SCI "Working Through Your Grief" series, a woman about seventy years of age rose to share her own grief experience. She told that following her husband's death, she had received no help from her congregation. After some months of growing loneliness and deepening depression, she made a list of other widows in the community. She invited them to her home and learned that each felt isolated since her husband's death. They had met regularly for seven months. As she finished her story, she looked around at the eighty people gathered for the seminar, among whom were all the community pastors. She challenged them to learn from the experience of her group and to join together to develop a community-wide grief program.

Joan and Mark Simmonds

A couple in their mid-sixties, Joan and Mark joined a grief support group in its third session. Apart from introducing themselves and informing the group that they grieved their daughter's death, they made few contributions in the ensuing three sessions. Mark was more reticent than Joan. During the seventh session, one of the co-leaders asked members if their grief was accompanied by anger and, if so, whether that made it more difficult to work through bereavement. Joan turned to Mark abruptly and asked her husband what he did with all his anger! Immobilized by her question, Mark did not respond.

Joan turned back to the group and shared their story: Their daughter, Margaret, had an acute form of leukemia. When Margaret's husband was unable to cope with her illness, he divorced her, and she returned to her parents' home with her two children—twins, age four. Joan and Mark cared for their dying daughter, lavishing love on their twin granddaughters. During Margaret's long illness, her former husband remarried, divorced his second wife after a brief marriage, and then remarried.

Although Joan and Mark believed they would be able to face Margaret's death when it came, they were still unprepared for the intensity of their pain. In the midst of their anguish, the girls' father arrived to take custody of the twins. The grandparents found some consolation in the tenderness and sensitivity of the twins' new step-mother, but their anger toward their former son-in-law knew no bounds. They abruptly left their Presbyterian congregation, in which Joan was an elder, hurt by what they experienced as God's abandonment of Margaret and themselves.

They had seen the newspaper announcement of the grief-support group and thought it might help them "get over the grief." Joan shared with the group the bitterness in their lives. Facing her husband, she said that they had been unable to focus their bitterness until that moment. She burst out: "We haven't been able to talk to each other about our anger, and it feels like it is killing us."

Joan and Mark attended three more weekly sessions, during which they began to verbalize their pain and focus their anger, while also listening to other group members and affirming their efforts to express their grief. They informed the group at the next meeting that they had worshiped at their church the previous Sunday, that they felt ready to "get on with their lives," and then took their leave from the group.

Resources exist in most communities which pastors and lay leaders can call upon for assistance in establishing grief-support groups. If the congregation does not include members with group-leadership skills and competence in grief support, arrangements might be made with a hospital, counseling center, or hospice to train and supervise members of the congregation, who could then assume the role of group facilitators. Hospice staffs usually include personnel who have group-leadership skills and are accustomed to training volunteers who are assigned to dying patients and their families. People with special grief needs may be referred to community-based grief-support programs such as Parents of Murdered Children or The Compassionate Friends.

Children's Grief-support Groups

The development of support groups for children and adolescents is just as important as the provision for adults' needs. In larger congregations, children's- and youth-education staff may be trained by professionals in the community to facilitate children's grief groups. Training for this function also can be undertaken by judicatory staff on an area-wide basis. Smaller congregations may share their resources in development of intercongregational grief groups, including interfaith groups.

The Unique Role of the Congregation

The emphasis by Worden and Davidson on the importance of socialization of grief has been slow to penetrate the practices of congregations. The needs of mourners ideally should be set in the context of the life of the community to which they belong. Mourners who are apt to withdraw into a private world of sorrow and remorse need to be recalled from their isolation by the needs of their social groups for their company and contribution. Bereaved individuals who pine for continuing support from families and communities, but experience its withdrawal, need the reassurance of continued affirmation and support from caregivers, who must overcome their hesitancy to share a mourner's pain in order to achieve the greater benefit of solidarity with people working through grief.

The tendency of congregants to privatize grief will be reversed, or at least modified, when their congregations address these concerns intentionally. The provision of grief-support groups is one starting point. The revisioning of funeral arrangements and liturgies is a second, but that must be addressed in a subsequent volume. Development of effective grief education is a third starting point.

The coordination of grief support and grief education is, or ought to be, a core ministry of the congregation. When a well-planned grief-education program which spans all ages and provides basic information regarding dying, death, and grief is in place, the effective support of grieving members will follow. Chapter 6 takes up this concern.

CHAPTER 6

Grief Education

Antony: *If you go on thus, you will kill yourself:*
         And 'tis not wisdom thus to second grief
         Against yourself.
Leonato: *I pray thee, cease thy counsel . . . for . . . men*
         Can counsel and speak comfort to that grief
         Which they themselves not feel, but, tasting it,
         Their counsel turns to passion. . . .
         Therefore give me no counsel:
         My griefs cry louder than advertisement.
                    MUCH ADO ABOUT NOTHING V.i.1ff.

Critics of psychotherapists contend that they give too much attention to individuals, instead of addressing the social conditions that inhibit or prevent individuals from leading full and productive lives. Christopher Lasch points out that this criticism is not recent, having been made by Erich Fromm, Johann Reich, and Otto Rank.[1] Donald Browning pointed out this issue in an article in 1966. He referred to the claim of "leading theoreticians of public ministry" who maintained that representatives of the pastoral-counseling movement were more concerned with one-to-one relationships with their (middle class) clients than with ethical concerns arising from dehumanizing social structures that lay at the root of personal crises.[2] Lasch argues that while care of the individual is the content of pastoral care, individual ministry cannot properly be separated from care of the community.[3]

Applying this thesis to community attitudes to public experiences and expressions of grief, care of the community involves dealing with underlying problems of social pathology that lead to avoidance of issues related to dying and death, resulting in grief avoidance, which harms both society and its individual members. The system—that is, the community—is at fault. Lasch refers to a 1937 paper by sociologist Lawrence Frank, in which Frank wrote of society as "the patient," suggesting that "the concept of a sick society in need of treatment is far more illuminating than conceptions stressing human volition, autonomy, and individual responsibility."[4] Yet both aspects of the problem must be addressed: Social scientists and therapists should be concerned with societal ills that lead to stresses in individuals' lives, as well as with the proper care of those individuals who are maimed by the consequences of those very ills.

Christian congregations, as the loci of pastoral care, are obligated to support individuals and families stricken by life's tragedies, but also should attend to those factors, which, when neglected, leave individuals less able to work through those crises. This applies particularly to the needs of bereaved members. If we expand Lasch's concept somewhat, not only individuals, but segments of a community bear responsibility for the health of the whole.

With respect to grief response, congregations are faced with the challenge to develop more effective support of mourning members, while at the same time educating their members to respond more effectively to grief when it breaks into their own lives. A single congregation may not be able to alter societal trends, but if fundamental changes in the way we deal with dying and death are introduced throughout the church, significant progress may be made toward healthier societal responses. Such progress would be communicated to individuals and families, preparing them to meet grief when a loved one dies. The provision of effective grief education that spans all ages is an effective way to address both individual and societal ills inherent in our death-denying culture.

The opportunity for grief education is inherent in every act of grief ministry. Jane's support of Mary Gibson becomes an opportunity for both Mary and Jane to continue learning about bereavement and how to fashion and accept grief support. Mary's visits with Jane create the possibility for Mary to understand the extent of the grief she is experiencing, and her need to work through not only John's death but the earlier bankruptcy, relocation, Elizabeth's divorce, and any other losses and changes that may have intensified her bereavement. Had Mary been aware before John's death of the nature and extent of grief, she might have been better able to complete the tasks of mourning with a greater degree of self-awareness, and perhaps faced a lesser risk of her grief deepening into clinical depression.

The retired couple who returned from Corpus Christi to Houston stated that they would not have been so shaken by the fear of "going crazy" if they had been aware of the link between relocation and grief. The father of the brilliant young pathologist might have been able to work through his rage at his son's premature death if, as part of his education for life, he had been aware that anger was both understandable and not unexpected. People who anticipate events may be better prepared to face and work through them when they occur.

In respect to providing grief *education*, there is a *pastoral* intent and consequence in the provision of education opportunities for all ages in the congregation. When pastoral care is shaped into a total program of support and education in the congregation, grief ministry to a particular bereaved family is then provided in the context of learning opportunities in which the whole family has already been involved.

Grief education should begin at the preschool level and continue as children come face to face with death and want to know more about dying, death, and grief. Mandy's "grief education" probably began much earlier than the age of four, because her parents responded to their children's questions about dying and death as they arose. During Mandy's fourth year, her mother, a physician, was assigned to her hospital's Life Flight staff. Following a flight on the previous day to a freeway wreck scene, Mandy's parents had discussed the scene the Life Flight crew had found. A passenger in one car had been killed. As I drove Mandy to her school the next morning, she turned to me and asked:

"Pa, are you going to die?"

"Yes, Mandy," I replied. "Every living thing and person dies."

"Pa, I don't want you to die," Mandy said.

"When we get old, each person dies. But sometimes, people, even young people, die in accidents or because they were very sick. Then that is very sad for the ones who love them."

"Pa, are you old?"

"Not yet, Mandy!" I replied. "I have lots of things I need to do before then. But I guess sometimes we need to remember that people, including ourselves and those we love, will die. Then we are sad for a while. People learn that, gradually, the sad, lonely times go away, even though they seem to last for a long time."

"Oh, Pa, I would be sad forever," Mandy replied.

Many adults think that children should be protected from talking about dying and death, that such experiences are too painful. Yet children cannot be protected from these realities, and it is often the adults who are unable to confront dying and death. In a session with twenty-five junior-high students on the subject of dying and death, I found that five students had experienced the death of a family member during the previous twelve months.

When I mentioned that statistic in another setting, a first-grade teacher was motivated to ask the children in her class if any had known a person who had died in the previous year. Of twenty-two children, nineteen mentioned the name of a family member who had died. Add to the deaths of family members or neighbors that of a teacher or student at school and the images of violent death on the TV screen, and it is impossible for children to avoid or ignore the reality that grief is an integral aspect of human life.

The question is not whether we should educate children regarding grief, but the kind and quality of education we do offer. Even if we avoid any mention of dying, death, or grief, by that avoidance, we are making statements about how our particular family or community responds to death. When children's enquiries about death are avoided, we compound a child's anxieties by our reluctance and uncertainty, leaving the unmistakable message that these are matters too dire to face.

Earl Grollman cites Dr. Jerome Bruner, director of the Harvard Center for Cognitive Studies, "who begins with the hypothesis than any subject can be explained effectively in an intellectually honest form to any child at any stage of development."[5] Fred Rogers of "Mr. Rogers' Neighborhood," puts it another way: "Anything human is mentionable, and anything mentionable can be manageable." He acknowledges that it is difficult to discuss dying and death with children, but because they do not understand what death is all about, children need adults who can talk about it with them.[6]

Grief education is thus the necessary corollary to effective grief support. It is as important to provide the opportunity for children and adults to learn about grief as it is to minister to people in mourning. Lawrence LeShan suggests that two of the best-kept secrets of the twentieth century are that everyone suffers and that suffering can be used for learning and growth.[7] Experiences of grief create the possibility of processing grief at both cognitive and affective levels, creating the potential for growing self-understanding, ability to develop and foster intimacy, and, ultimately, to survive losses of significant relationships.

Educating Parents and Teachers

Child-rearing studies indicate that education of children takes place at two levels: that of the child who is growing in self and general knowledge, and that of the adult educator—parent or teacher. For example, much of the research focusing on teaching and applying discipline indicates that a fundamental error has been made by many investigators. Jane Brody reports that "discipline is being applied to children when it should be applied to their parents (and teachers)." Brody cites researchers who believe that most parents lack a good grasp of what to do when problems arise. Their responses are not always helpful, and when they rely on their emotions, they often end up feeling guilty.

Studies are indicating, for example, that beyond the importance of combining expressions of love with setting appropriate limits, there is a greater variety of skills and methods than has been recognized. Disciplinary occasions differ, and children are different. Parents must develop styles of relating to children with which they are comfortable, but before parents can become effective disciplinarians, "they must first learn how to manage their own anger, solve problem situations, and give and get support from others."[8]

This model can be applied to teaching and learning how to cope with grief. Parents first must be aware of the grief process, understand its likely impact on their own lives, and develop effective means to work through their own grief, before they can assist their children in this process. Both the commissions and omissions of parents in grief education and grief care are likely to impose a more of less permanent pattern of grief response on their children—permanent, that is, unless later reformed. A simple illustration demonstrates the importance of this issue—namely, including children in family funerals.

Don accompanied his parents, Robert and Norma, to the funeral of his grandfather. Following the church service, the family rode in the traditional funeral procession to the cemetery. Don, age three, was curious about the service, their subsequent destination, and what would happen there. His parents answered his questions factually. It was clear that adults in the service, particularly Don's grandmother, were sad. Robert and Norma talked about loved ones' sadness when a family member dies. Older adults in the family questioned the wisdom of including Don in the funeral—"a funeral is no place for children." But Don observed the range of feelings expressed by members of his family, and he did so in a safe environment; he noted that his parents were sad but that the sadness was not frightening nor disabling.

If, on the other hand, children are excluded from adults' experiences of grief, a very different message is learned. A child's pattern of grief response is reinforced each time the exclusion is repeated. If we develop grief education curriculum for children K through 12, we must do so in the context of adequate training for adults.*

A Grief Education Program for Adults

Regardless of the quality and effectiveness of grief education curriculum and methods used in the classroom or church school, it is unlikely that children will develop adequate coping skills to work through grief unless these values also are communicated in the home and classroom. We hope that adults who are to undertake the primary teaching role in helping children cope with dying, death and grief will have developed healthy, effective ways to work through their own griefs. Congregations are ideally situated to assist parents to develop their own understanding of bereavement and mourning, so that in turn they may teach their children healthy ways to respond to grief.

Sam Keen discloses the inadequacy of the models he acquired as a child for dealing with experiences of loss and change as an adult. He reflects on the development of males in his North American culture:

> Most of us learned that real men were supposed to control their feelings. From childhood onward we hard that "men don't cry." We learned to work hard, take a lot of punishment, and not bitch about it. . . . No pain, no gain. That's the right stuff. . . . In order to be free, the prison

---

*Hereafter, the term *adults* will refer to parents, teachers, and other significant adults whose regular activities include caregiving roles relative to dependent children.

doors must be flung open and the imprisoned feelings invited into the commonwealth of the self. Since boys are taught not to cry, men must learn to weep. After a man passes through arid numbness, he comes to a tangled jungle of grief and unnamed sorrow. *The path to a manly heart runs through the valley of tears. . . . Men have much to mourn before they can be reborn.* (emphasis added)[9]

James Nelson also describes growing up in a culture which taught that "big boys don't cry." When, at twenty-one, his father died, he returned from his army post for the funeral but refused to see his father's body. He wanted to remember him in health, not in death: "Only years later did I realize how symbolic it was that I chose to attend my dad's funeral in uniform. I could not really grieve, for that would have expressed the weakness and vulnerability which I had learned to deny. It took twenty-five years and some good therapy before I could get in touch with my grief and anger. And now I know how alienated I was from a whole range of bodily feelings all of those years."[10]

If the two sets of adults who spend most time with children—parents or guardians and day-school teachers—are often ill-prepared to recognize, understand, and respond to their own grief processes and needs, they will be equally ill-equipped to respond to children's anxieties and fears about death and separation.

This lack of awareness is portrayed in the responses of a middle-school principal to whom a young widow appealed for help for her twelve-year-old son. Her husband had died six months earlier, and her son's behavior's indicated his inability to accept his father's death. She described his acting-out behaviors at home and asked the principal to consult with staff teachers, so they would be aware that inappropriate behaviors at school were related to his grief. The principal terminated the phone call with the comment that he did not know why they were having the conversation.

In the conversation with junior-high students, in which I learned that five of the group of twenty-five had experienced a death in the family, one student reported that her brother had been murdered on his college campus twelve months earlier.

Realizing that the first anniversary was just two days away, I suggested, "Beth, I guess you did not feel like coming to school today?"

"No," replied Beth.

"And you won't be at school Thursday?"

Again, she replied, "No." The session ended, and three teachers ran across the room.

They burst out, "Now we can understand her behavior over the past few weeks. Her school grades have gone from straight A's to C's. Her whole attitude has been impossible!" When I asked them if they had not expected that this anniversary week would be a difficult time for Beth, they looked helplessly at one another and acknowledged that they had not recognized the possible link between her brother's murder and Beth's changed demeanor a year later.

Stories reflecting similar failures to understand the impact of unresolved grief in the lives of children have been repeated too often in cities from Portland, Oregon, to Tallahassee, Florida, and from to Portland, Main, to Sacramento, California, for them to be isolated instances unrepresentative of the mainstream of American life. When teachers' and parents' stories are reinforced by the realization that few pastors have been trained to provide pastoral care to grieving children, and less than 2 percent of congregations report a self-conscious, intentional grief-support program to families with dependent children, the failure becomes monstrous.

Teaching Children About Dying, Death, and Grieving

We are entering an area into which very few people appear to have ventured; therefore we must start from the beginning and feel our way forward. Two dimensions of the problem require attention: The fashioning of grief-education programs for children must proceed hand-in-hand with similar programs for their caregivers. Fortunately, we are not entirely without models, though their availability seems to go largely unnoticed. Following our seminar in one Midwest community, a teacher of children with special-education needs wrote that each of the eight teachers who attended had gained insight that will impact thousands of children throughout the school district. Another commented that following a colleague's murder, she had talked with the teacher's class and invited them to draw pictures that expressed their grief. The pictures were then compiled into a book of memories for their teacher. This exercise was complemented by the use of children's books about dying and death.

She added, "I have often questioned my effectiveness in helping them to deal with their grief. The seminar confirmed my philosophy of fostering an open communication in talking about feelings associated with death, loss, and grief, allowing the children to teach us what their needs are."[11]

A colleague shared with me the report of a national teachers' conference at which a classroom teacher described how she worked through the death of a student in her sixth-grade class. Following Anne's death, the students were helped to make a decision regarding Anne's desk. Four options were identified by the class: They could leave Anne's desk in its place, unoccupied; another child could be assigned to the desk; the desk could be removed to the back of the classroom; or the desk could be removed from the room. The class decided to leave Anne's desk in its place, unoccupied, until the end of the semester.

When the teacher asked what should be done with Anne's books and papers in the desk and on the wall display boards, they decided to keep Anne's belongings in her desk and on the walls. At the end of the semester, a group of Anne's friends would deliver the books and papers to her parents.

Following the presentation of this story to the teachers' conference, a teacher in her mid-sixties thanked the previous teacher for the account of how Anne's death had been handled. She remarked that when she had been in grade six, a fellow student had died. The following morning, the student's desk had been removed from the classroom, and no mention was ever made about the child's death. She expressed her gratitude that teachers now knew that there are other, more sensitive and creative ways to respond to the death of a child or teacher.

Similar gratitude is reflected in a letter from a Midwest school district, from which representatives had attended the "A Child's View of Grief" seminar. The letter stated that a teacher in one of the district schools had died two days after the seminar. Teachers who otherwise would not have felt adequate to meet the situation were able to assist children in her classroom to accept and begin to work through her death.

How Do Children Learn from Life Experiences?

In order to develop a grief-education program for very young children, we need to know how children learn. Early in toddlerhood, children begin to distinguish reality from fantasy. If we recall that even in adulthood, we may be apt to take refuge in fantasy to escape the "slings and arrows of outrageous fortune," at least temporarily, we realize that this task, begun in childhood, is never really quite complete! Preschool children also enter a phase of cognitive development integrally related to language development. These advances are shaped by the families and cultures of which they are members, as L. Joseph Stone and Joseph Church have pointed out:

> Language as it is handed down to children may liberate their thinking but may also constrict it by embalming experience in stale formulas and cliches, by providing false or non-existent conceptual entities and explanations, by shuning interesting topics like sex and death off into the realm of euphemism or the unspeakable, and by deceiving children into thinking they have understood something just because they have labeled it and catalogued it. At its best, though, language can free children's thinking by providing them with useful ideas, forms, and operations. [12]

As children's knowledge of themselves and their world expands, so too do their fears. Their awareness of sickness and death is not a product of abstract thinking but of the experiences they now confront—for example, illnesses or deaths of family members (often of grandparents), those of classmates or neighbors, or deaths observed on the TV screen. The manner in which these concrete events are internalized and become parts of children's phenomenological worlds—that is, the way they receive and integrate new knowledge about their worlds—is formed in the context of the family and culture of which they are members.

Thus, the way a child's family confronts dying and death will determine to a large extent what he or she internalizes about grief experiences. Factors and influences that shape how and what the child learns include: How open—or closed—are parents to discussion of dying and death between themselves and with their children; the manner in which these subjects are discussed or avoided; and the broader cultural mores concerning dying and death to which the family adheres. The attitudes children adopt in turn determine what decisions later will be made, and how those decisions about dying and death will be reached.

Added to the ways adults model the processes by which they face dying and death, are other experiences in children's lives: the deaths of family members; the mode of death—whether sudden, due to chronic illness, suicide, or homicide; the proximity of the relationship to the child—for example, the death of a parent or sibling, or deaths of friends' parents. The intensity and duration of children's grief experiences will be affected also by the degree of security they have in their relationships with significant adults, their participation in or exclusion from caring for dying family members, and the individual child's need to deny or hide feelings.

Essentials in a Grief-education Curriculum

Children learn early in life that they "sorrow," or are "sad" when separated from someone to whom they are attached, or from an object in which they have made a significant investment. Even before they have developed appropriate language skills, they are aware that separation is painful.[13] They experience the feelings evoked by *grief*, though they may not yet understand the meaning of the term itself. They are learning a fundamental reality—namely, that life consists of continuous experiences of loss and change. They are learning, in fact, that life may bump them from one grief experience to another, and they will need the tools by which to process these events, lest, in Bowlby's terms, their inability to cope leads to the development of "defensive processes [that] once set in motion are apt to stabilize and persist."[14]

A curriculum designed to assist children in this learning process must not only provide information about the grief process on which they are embarked, but must do so in an environment in which it is safe to explore both the cognitive and affective components that constitute adaptation to grief. Attention must therefore be given to the need to validate children's feelings evoked by loss. This is important, since it is one of the tragedies of contemporary society that, for many people, being in touch with feelings has been negatively reinforced.

Validation of children's feelings is a positive reinforcement, particularly if the feelings are uncomfortable or distressing. For example, many children have learned from adults that it is "wrong" to be angry. It is an even greater tragedy when children are taught that anger is a "sin" and, as a consequence, bear an unnecessary burden of guilt if they feel anger toward their surviving parent or the parent who has died.

Eda LeShan, in a book written for children struggling to work through the death of a parent, describes the feelings they are likely to experience. Disbelief that a parent has died may give way to terror and, in turn, to angry feelings. Bereaved children may wonder how someone who loved them could abandon them. They might think, "What a terrible thing to do to a little child." Such feelings may leave a residue of guilt: "Maybe in some way this is (my) fault. Did (I) make too much noise while Daddy was sick? Did Mom get sick because (I) made her work too hard?"[15]

LeShan tells her readers that she wrote her book because, when her mother was four years old, LeShan's grandmother had died, but LeShan's mother was not told the truth—relatives felt that she was too young. When she asked where her mother was, she was told her mother was sick and had gone to the country. Observing that all the relatives were sad, LeShan's mother decided that her mother did not love her and had left her because she was a bad girl. Even though she learned the truth from strangers she had overheard talking about her mother's death, she carried her painful memories all her life. LeShan tells us she learned from her mother "that a child can live through *anything*, so long as he or she is told the truth and is allowed to share with loved ones the natural feelings people have when they are suffering."[16]

When to Talk About Dying and Death

Caregivers really have little choice if there has been a recent death in a child's family. Parents need to face that directly with each child, and one of the congregation's more important pastoral functions may be to assist parents to anticipate this need and prepare to meet it. There are many other opportunities to discuss death. The death of a family pet or a bird found in the yard provides the opportunity to discuss dying and death at a time when everyone is less emotionally involved. Some children show considerable curiosity about dead animals and insects and wish to examine them closely and ask questions. It is their way of learning about death and is an important moment to grasp that all living things have a lifetime which ends in death.

Honest, unemotional, and simple answers are called for. If talking with a very young child, remember he or she learns by increments. Children absorb a little of what they hear, asking the same questions again and again, gradually extending their knowledge base and growing familiar with concepts. If Bess skips away calling, "Well, I'm never going to die," she should not be contradicted, and adults should not imagine their efforts at education are wasted. Patience and sensitivity will make it easier for her to return and ask her questions again.

Robert Kastenbaum notes that the efforts of adults to protect children from death is an understandable impulse, but such protection does not meet their needs: "We can provide more emotional security to our children with a better command of the facts and acquaintance with guidelines derived from intensive direct experiences."[17] Many adults have much to learn—or relearn—in order to compensate for the deficits in childhood education. Effective grief education in early childhood may serve a preventive function, preparing young children to expect, and to meet and resolve their experiences of loss and change. In due course, they will be able to provide more effective grief support and grief education to their own children.

One aspect of grief education that has gained increasing acceptance is the class excursion to a funeral home, through which children are oriented to the procedures followed when a person dies. Many funeral directors are accustomed to explaining their procedures in terms appropriate to children's stages of readiness. Children benefit because they are enabled to explore dying and death as part of their learning processes. Another positive result is the familiarization of funeral practices in childhood, as a foundation for dealing as adults with the deaths of family members. Church-school grief curriculum should also include such opportunities, which may be enriched by the involvement of the children's pastor, who will set the visit in the context of their faith community's interpretation of dying and death, and the funeral.

Care of a terminally ill family member may be an opportunity to assist children to face the reality of death. Children are more likely to be harmed than reassured by their exclusion from this experience. Kastenbaum elaborates on how the support of children in the dying member's family is inherently tied to deepening their understanding of what is happening, so that their fears can be identified and eased. His guidelines include:

1. Listen to what children say about themselves and their environments and observe their behaviors. A patient and attentive response to children's concerns will assist adults in sensing the perceptions and misperceptions about dying and death.

2. Avoid "one big tell-all." That is, issues related to dying and death should be dealt with as they arise, at each child's level of readiness. "This does not mean that parents should be poised to jump on a death dialogue opportunity. It is more natural and effective to include death as one of the many topics that adults and children discuss together." Adults are more likely to be able to respond more effectively if such discussions occur when they are not themselves caught up in their own grief: "Combine a child who has been kept ignorant about death with an adult who is grief stricken, and you have something less than the most desirable situation."[18]

3. A child's response will emerge over time, and may be delayed longer than adults' responses. Changes in children's regular habits may indicate they are having difficulty coping with their bereavement.

4. If children are removed from the family and sent to stay elsewhere, they may be left struggling with the feeling of being excluded. This may cost them the opportunity to learn from the situation how to participate in the family's response. Their continued involvement may also provide insight into their perceptions and misperceptions about dying and grief.

5. Simple, direct language and explanations, accessibility to parents and other significant family members, awareness of each individual child's needs, and the continued support of adults, even if a child's behavior disturbs or angers them, are also important, both in caring for children and in helping them learn effective ways of responding to grief.

Donna O'Toole supports the position that children should be assisted to learn from their own experiences of grief. In her grief-education curriculum *Growing Through Grief,* she states that childhood grief education introduces opportunities to better prepare children with skills and knowledge they will need as adults.[19] Subsequently, when a child experiences the death of a loved one, support of the child in the context of previous learning processes, which have provided at least rudimentary skills for confronting the experience of bereavement that has now occurred.

A Congregation-based Program

Since many families in any community have no connection with a congregation, a congregation-based program may be offered as a community service. The following steps may be followed by a single congregation (or as an interfaith activity by a group of congregations):

1. Develop a curriculum that the church-education staff will provide through its all-age program.[20] Present the concept to the parish-congregational council for adoption. If a community-wide project is envisioned, convene a program committee drawn from community agencies—for example, congregations, school districts, private schools—to plan a one-day seminar through which to introduce the project. Announce the program through the media, and solicit opportunities to discuss the project with media representatives.

2. Invite parents to attend the seminar, explaining that it will equip them to recognize and be better able to work through grief in their own lives, as preparation to enable them to assist their children in coping with grief.

3. Train leaders who will serve as facilitators of small groups of parents throughout the seminar.

4. Seminar program (10:00 A.M. through 4:00 P.M.):

Introduction of seminar objectives and program [10 min.]

Introduction to the grief process, with particular reference to helping children cope with grief (materials may be drawn from chapters 3 and 4 above). [90 min.]

Place parents in groups of 6 or 8 and present the following topics for discussion:

What was your earliest experience of grief? How well did you resolve it? How did adults help (or not help) you? If your children faced this experience, how would you help them to face it? What do you need from your (congregation, school) to help you help your children? [90 min.]

Reconvene the participants and identify, by issues, the content of discussions in the small groups. [30 min.]

Introduce an outline of the K through 12 grief-education curriculum which the congregation will provide for its families. [30 min.]

Wrap up, and inquire whether parents would value the provision of grief-support groups for both adults and children. [30 min.]

The notion of congregational and secular educators working together on this project has much to commend it. We have much to teach one another and much to share with people of all ages. In an area which society in general has long avoided entering, congregation and day-school should be in conversation concerning the most effective and caring manner in which to develop and implement grief education curriculum. The seminar outline suggested above can bring together congregational and secular education personnel in a way that maximizes the community's total resources. Moreover, cooperation between parents and congregational and secular education staffs may ensure that the fullest level of care is available to assist grieving children to work through the tasks of mourning. The seminar outline above is suggested as a starting point for parents who have not given serious thought to these matters or introduced them in their families.

The next step is the provision of "continuing-education" opportunities for parents, to coincide with the introduction of child and adolescent grief education in the programs of the congregation. A session on practical steps parents may take may also be included. For example, parents of dependent children can be challenged to ensure that they have made provision for the welfare of their children in the event of the deaths of both parents. Married couples who have not faced openly with each other the questions about how the survivor would manage in the event of the death of the spouse may be assisted to begin that conversation. For example, couples may discuss preparing other family members, development of an estate-planning program, and preparation of a list of actions that would need to be taken when the first partner dies.

Education for the Tasks of Mourning at Mid-life and Beyond

Grief education is important for people of all ages, if the widely held belief is accurate that 50 percent of adults have not made wills, and an unknown but considerable number must face the death of their life partners unprepared for its consequences. A few data from statistical information gathered from a variety of research programs demonstrates the scope of the issues that are at stake for adults in the middle and later years. For example, an analysis of census returns indicates that . . .

. . . The average age at which Americans are widowed is 56;

. . . 50% of women over 65 are widows.

In 1983 there were approximately 11 million widows and 2 million widowers. Also in 1983 . . .

. . . 77.9% of African American women 55 or older were widowed;
. . . 67.6% of white women 55 or older were widowed;
. . . 20.6% of white men 55 or older were widowed.

In 1969, the Life Insurance Management Association surveyed 1,744 widows whose husbands had died before they were 65, to ascertain the economic impact of widowhood and the way widows cope with their life changes. The study found that most widows needed help to adjust to their changed status, particularly regarding legal, financial, and employment matters, and that support from families, friends, and clergy did not meet long-term needs. A similar study undertaken in 1985 by Iowa State University interviewed 84 widowers between age 60 and 91. The researchers concluded that widowers were better able to adjust to their new status when they had a male confidant (rather than depending on children, siblings, or woman confidant), and were part of a support system through which they could form close friendships.

Data such as these indicate that the provision of adequate support for people bereaved at mid-life or beyond may be instrumental in enabling the person in mourning to work through grief. Preparation through grief education that may prepare this population to complete the tasks of mourning is the logical next step to complement effective pastoral care. As with adolescents and young adults, a curriculum for older adults will begin with the presentation of the elements of the grief process, always in a context that encourages participants to explore their own grief experiences. The teaching device sketched in chapters 2 and 3 starts with a didactic presentation, but moves quickly to an experiential mode, as group members present their own experiences in illustration of the respective components of the model, and the means they have adopted to work through them.

It is important for younger parents to consider and prepare for the eventuality of the death of one or both life partners, and to include their children at levels appropriate to their development and maturity. As people age, it is equally important to continue these preparations and, like one's will, to update them regularly. Many people enter adulthood in what is still a death-denying society. Provision of grief-education seminars as regular elements in adult-education programs for members in their middle or later years will ease the transition from a culture in which such discussions were avoided, to one in which they are part of continuing-education programs that will enable individuals to live their lives to the fullest.

Ancient cultures may be our teachers in this process. Genesis closes with Jacob's preparation of his family for his death, followed by similar preparations made by Joseph (40:28-33; 50:22-25). Moses prepared the twelve tribes for his death: "I am now one hundred twenty years old. I am no longer able to get about, and the Lord has told me 'You shall not cross over this Jordan.' . . . The Lord said to Moses, 'Your time to die is near; call Joshua and present yourselves in the tent of meeting, so that I may commission him.' " (Deut. 31:2, 14*a*).

Whereupon Moses recited the great deeds of God in behalf of Israel (32:1-43), blessed the tribes, and climbed Mount Pisgah in Moab, where he died. The telling and retelling of these events throughout Israel's history not only serves the purpose of passing the tradition from one generation to the next, but does so in a context that stresses the ordinariness, the normalcy, of this process.

Caring for a Dying Person Can Be a Learning Experience

During the course of a family member's protracted illness, the two complementary factors of loving, compassionate care of the dying person, and the opportunity for other members to grow through this experience ought always to be kept in balance. Much has been learned from the more formal setting of hospice programs, and from the personal reflections of individual patients and caregivers.

Hospice regimens emphasize the principle of keeping as much control over life processes and decisions as possible in the hands of the dying person. Goals include pain control; remission of symptoms, which contributes to the patient's comfort; establishing the patient's wishes regarding a Living Will or similar document; affording the patient a sense of security and protection in his or her environment; opportunities for leave-taking with the people most important to the patient; and opportunities for experiencing the final moments in a way that is meaningful to the patient.[21]

These objectives are shaped by the desire to provide comfort and consolation to the patient and family alike. In the process of providing *care* for their patient, family members are learning to face dying and death. For example, family members are afforded opportunities to discuss dying, death, and the feelings evoked by these events.

Learning About Dying from People Living with AIDS

Much is being learned from the growing body of experience emerging from care of people with HIV disease. Early in the course of the epidemic, people with AIDS rejected the notion that they were "*dying* from AIDS" and began to insist on being treated as "people *living* with AIDS." At the same time, they have been teaching the well community how to die. This image was captured in a series of articles in an issue of *The Journal of Pastoral Care* which focused on pastoral care to people living with AIDS.

In discussion with Elizabeth Goss about her ministry to people with HIV disease, we discovered that our experiences were remarkably similar. Both of us had served as chaplains on hospital oncology units; now we were colleagues caring for AIDS patients. We reflected that neither of us had routinely discussed dying, planning the funeral, or disposition of remains with other terminally ill patient populations, but were now customarily raising these issues with people with AIDS. In her article, Goss noted:

> People with AIDS become preoccupied with dying and death. In my experience, this occurs with greater intensity and frequency than I have observed with any other patient population. The unexpected aspects of this preoccupation are the lack of morbidity with which dying and death are explored by patients, the ease I have experienced in raising these issues if patients do not, and patients' comfort when I do so. . . . As I reflect on this phenomenon, it still feels out of place when I think of ministering to cancer patients or other terminally ill patients, yet the most natural and appropriate step with people with AIDS.[22]

Goss then asks why the subject of dying and death is taboo with some patient populations, but an open door with others? Goss and I concluded that "something different" is happening as we minister to people living and dying with AIDS. In an earlier period in the development of pastoral ministry to the sick, it could be argued that "everything which is done at the time of death is done for those who still live and feel."[23] Now it is clear that such sentiments were based on a too-narrow perception of the process of dying and death: "Death is at stake in dying, and people dying from diseases resulting from HIV infection are intensely aware of their deaths. For the most part, they are determined to be actors in their *deaths*, and so are helped to die."[24]

Whereas once it could be stated with some force that funeral liturgies were intended to assist the living to act out and work through their deep feelings of grief, "such images may apply to all in the family circle involved in imminent death, and usually, in the case of death due to HIV disease, including the dying person, who not only does not want to be left out of these events, but may need to orchestrate them!"[25] As a consequence, I suggested, the awareness of the proximity of dying and death on the part of people with AIDS, and their readiness to discuss frankly their comprehension, feelings, and plans concerning dying and death, including funeral planning, have created a situation unique in the annals of the pastoral-care movement.[26]

This unique situation can be summarized in the notion that we have the opportunity and privilege of learning about dying from people living with AIDS. The pastoral-care movement has long emphasized the role of patients as "living human documents," and pastoral students are challenged to recognize and acknowledge patients as their teachers. That learning model may be extended to including the dying. As growing numbers of clergy and laypeople care for people with HIV disease through dying, and remain with them through death, death is being robbed of its sting, and the grave of its victory.

NOTES

INTRODUCTION

1. Colleen McCullough, *The Grass Crown* (New York: William Morrow & Co., 1991), p. 234.
2. Ibid., p. 331.
3. Ibid., p. 421.
4. See, for example, Samuel Southard, *Death and Dying: A Bibliographical Survey* (New York: Greenwood, 1991). With more than 8,000 references, Southard's is one of the most complete and thoroughly annotated references in the field of thanatology. He documents theological and philosophical contributions among a vast array of texts. See also *The Dictionary of Pastoral Care and Counseling* (Nashville: Abingdon Press, 1990) and Michael A. Simpson, *Dying, Death, and Grief: A Critical Bibliography* (Pittsburgh: University Press, 1987).
5. Michael Simpson, *Dying, Death, and Grief* (New York: Plenum, 1979), p. vii.
6. J. William Worden, *Grief Counseling and Grief Therapy*, 2nd ed. (New York: Springer Publishing Co., 1991).

CHAPTER 1—Understanding Grief

1. Juvenal, *The Sixteen Satires*, x, Trans. Peter Green (Harmondsworth, Middlesex, England: Penguin Books, 1967), 1.173.
2. Fulke Greville, "Elegy on the Death of Sir Philip Sydney."
3. Richard Hooker, in Samuel Johnson, *Preface to the English Dictionary*, Vol. 1 (London: W. Strahan/AMS Press, 1967).
4. Robert Southey, "The Curse of Kemaha," xv, 12.
5. W. E. Aytoun, "The Island of the Scots," *Victorian Literature: Poetry*, ed. Donald J. Gray and G. B. Tennyson (New York: Macmillan, 1976), xii.
6. Annie Dillard, *Pilgrim at Tinker Creek* (New York: Harper's Magazine Press, 1974), p. 89.
7. Josef Israel, "Alleen op de wereld, ook wel Niets meer of Alleen," trans., "Alone in the World, in other words, Nothing More Left, or Alone," ca. 1881; The van Gogh Museum, Amsterdam.

8. Leo Tolstoy, *The Death of Ivan Ilych* (New York: Penguin Books, 1960), p. 134.
9. See, for example, Fred G. Gealy, "The Biblical Understanding of Death," *Pastoral Psychology* (June 1963), pp. 33-40; Lloyd R. Bailey, "Death as a Theological Problem in the Old Testament," *Pastoral Psychology* (November 1971), pp. 20-32.
10. Sigmund Freud, "Mourning and Melancholia," *The Standard Edition of the Complete Works of Sigmund Freud XIV* (London: Hogarth Press, 1957). See also *Collected Papers IV* (New York: Basic Books, 1959), pp. 288-317; 152-70.
11. Freud, *Standard Edition XX*, p. 258; *Collected Papers*, p. 163.
12. Ibid., p. 166.
13. Melanie Klein, "Mourning and its Relation to Manic-depressive States," *International Journal of Psycho-analysis* (April 1940), pp. 136-37.
14. Ibid., p. 143.
15. Erich Lindemann, "Symptomatology and Management of Acute Grief," *American Journal of Psychiatry* (September 1944), pp. 141-48.
16. Ibid., p. 145.
17. "Society Transactions," *Archives on Neurology and Psychiatry* (March 16, 1944), p. 324.
18. Lindemann, "Symptomatology," p. 141.
19. Ibid., p. 141.
20. Ibid., p. 143.
21. Ibid., p. 143.
22. Colin Murray Parkes, "Recent Bereavement as a Case of Mental Illness," *British Journal of Psychiatry* 110 (1964), pp. 198-204.
23. Colin Murray Parkes, *Bereavement: Studies in Grief in Adult Life* (New York: International Universities Press, 1972), p 5.
24. Ibid., p. 6.
25. Ibid., p. 10.
26. Ibid., p. 11.
27. Ibid., p. 11.
28. Peter Marris, *Loss and Change* (New York: Random House, 1974), p. 1.
29. Ibid., p. 4.
30. Ibid., p. 6.
31. Ibid., p. 11.
32. Ibid., p. 21.
33. J. William Worden, *Grief Counseling and Grief Therapy*, 2nd ed. (New York: Springer Publishing Co., 1991), p. ix.
34. Glen W. Davidson, *Living with Dying* (Minneapolis: Augsburg Publishing House, 1975).
35. Ibid., p. 28
36. Edgar N. Jackson, *Understanding Grief* (Nashville: Abingdon Press, 1957).
37. Ibid., p. 145. Not surprisingly, since in the 1950s pastoral ministry was generally accepted "by society" as a clergy rather than a congregational responsibility, Jackson identified the male ordained minister as the primary caregiver.
38. Ibid., p. 146.
39. Ibid., p. 154.
40. Ibid., p. 157.
41. Ibid., p. 161.
42. Granger E. Westberg, *Minister and Doctor Meet* (New York: Harper & Row, 1961).
43. Granger E. Westberg, *Good Grief* (Philadelphia: Fortress Press, 1962).
44. Ibid., p. 20.
45. See, for example, "Pastoral Psychology and the Funeral," *Pastoral Psychology* (November 1957); "The Funeral, Death, and Bereavement," *Pastoral Psychology* (June 1963); and "The Theology and Psychology of Death," *Pastoral Psychology* (June 1972).

46. R. Scott Sullender, "Three Theoretical Approaches to Grief," *The Journal of Pastoral Care* (December 1979), pp. 243-51.

47. See David K. Switzer, *The Dynamics of Grief* (Nashville: Abingdon Press, 1970), p. 83.

48. Ibid., p. 249.

49. Ibid., p. 251.

50. See Samuel Southard, *Death and Dying: A Bibliographical Survey* (New York: Greenwood, 1991).

51. Readers may request copies of both SCI video tapes—"Working Through Your Grief: Picking Up the Pieces" and "A Child's View of Grief"—by writing to Corporate Communications, SCI, Inc., P.O. Box 13548, Houston, Texas 77219-3548, or ordering by phone (713)525-9060. A third video, dealing with anticipatory grief, is in production.

CHAPTER 2—Working Through Grief

1. Reference is made to the work of Elisabeth Kubler-Ross for two reasons. First, she is one of the most widely recognized contributors to the literature on dying and death. Second, despite competent and comprehensive reviews of her work which present with accuracy her place in the field of thanatology, many people seem unaware of the critical questions that have been raised concerning the validity of her research and methodology, and fewer still have been able to free themselves from the misrepresentation by others of the so-called Five Stages.

2. Elisabeth Kubler-Ross, *On Death and Dying* (New York: Macmillan Publishing Co., 1969).

3. Robert White and Leroy Gathman, "The Syndrome of Ordinary Grief," *American Family Physician* (August 1973), pp. 97-104.

4. Granger E. Westberg, *Good Grief* (Philadelphia: Fortress Press, 1962), p. 20.

5. Sigmund Freud, *Collected Papers IV* (New York: Basic Books, 1959), p. 166.

6. Erich Lindemann, "Symptomatology and Management of Acute Grief," *American Journal of Psychiatry* (September 1944), p. 143.

7. J. William Worden, *Grief Counseling and Grief Therapy*, 1st ed. (New York: Springer Publishing Co., 1982), p. 11.

8. Ibid., pp. 11-12.

9. Peter Marris, *Loss and Change* (New York: Random House, 1974), p. 25.

10. Colin Murray Parkes, *Bereavement: Studies in Grief in Adult Life* (New York: International Universities Press, 1972), p. 52.

11. Geoffrey Gorer, *Death, Grief and Mourning in Contemporary Britain* (London: Cresset Press, 1965), p. 58.

12. Ronald H. Sunderland, "Working Through Your Grief," videotape (Houston: SCI Corp., 1989).

13. Westberg, *Good Grief*, p. 44.

14. Worden, *Grief Counseling*, p. 24.

15. See below for further references to The Compassionate Friends.

16. Eda LeShan, *Learning to Say Good-bye* (New York: Avon Books, 1988), pp. 40ff.

17. Eric Lindemann, "Symptomatology," p. 141ff.

18. Parkes, *Bereavement*, pp. 21, 39ff.

19. Marris, *Loss and Change*, p. 25ff.

20. Worden, *Grief Counseling*, p. 20.

21. Sunderland, "Working Through Your Grief." The videotape depicts a grief-support group as the members struggle to cope with their individual bereavements. As a

starting point in understanding the state of mind of bereaved people, the caregiver's attention is directed to Worden's chapter delineating "Normal Grief Reactions: Uncomplicated Mourning," *Grief Counseling*, pp. 19-23.

22. Alice Hoffman, *At Risk* (New York: G. P. Putnam's Sons, 1988).
23. Ibid., p. 54.
24. Ibid., p. 89.
25. Ibid., p. 207.
26. Edgar Jackson, *You and Your Grief* (New York: E. P. Dutton, 1962), p. 9.
27. Ibid., p. 14.
28. Worden, *Grief Counseling*, p. 28.
29. American Psychiatric Assoc., *Diagnostic and Statistical Manual of Mental Disorders (DSM III* 1980), p. 333.
30. "A Death in the Family," *Newsweek* (June 20, 1977), p. 89.
31. Stanley Weintraub, *Victoria* (New York: Truman Talley Books/E.P. Dutton, 1987), p. 305ff.
32. Worden, *Grief Counseling*, p. 48.
33. Jill K. Conway, *The Road from Coorain* (New York: Vintage Books, 1990), p. 72.
34. Ibid., p. 115.
35. Ibid., p. 212.
36. Ibid., p. 238.
37. Yorick Spiegel, *The Grief Process: Analysis and Counseling* (Nashville: Abingdon Press, 1977), p. 96.
38. N. W. Clerk (C. S. Lewis) *A Grief Observed* (Greenwich, Conn.: Seabury Press, 1963), pp. 13, 27, 37, 41-42.
39. Ibid., p. 41.

CHAPTER 3—Grief: Our Constant Companion

1. Erich Lindemann, "Symptomatology and Management of Acute Grief," *American Journal of Psychiatry* (September 1944), p. 147.
2. C. Murray Parkes, *Bereavement: Studies in Grief in Adult Life* (New York: International Universities Press, 1972), p. 11.
3. Marc Fried, "Grieving for a Lost Home," *The Urban Condition*, ed. Leonard Duhl (New York: Basic Books, 1963).
4. In presenting this material in a grief-education seminar, I draw a large circle on the board, add a segment representing bereavement (Fig. 12), then add such segments as retirement, divorce, relocation, amputation, and so on. After adding four or five segments, I invite participants to suggest further instances of loss or change which evoke grief. Final diagrams will vary with different groups, but usually there are common features, and the completed circle is likely to appear as shown in Fig. 13.
5. See William V. Arnold, *When Your Parents Divorce* (Philadelphia: Westminster Press, 1980), p. 25.
6. E. E. Whitehead and J. D. Whitehead, "Retirement," *Ministry with the Aging*, ed. William M. Clements (San Francisco: Harper & Row, 1981), p. 129.
7. Peter Marris, *Loss and Change* (New York: Random House, 1974), p. 148.
8. See Ronald H. Sunderland, "Prophetic Ministry: An Introduction," *The Pastor as Prophet*, ed. Earl E. Shelp and Ronald H. Sunderland (Philadelphia: Westminster Press, 1985), pp. 18ff.
9. Marris, *Loss and Change*, p. 150ff.
10. Colin Murray Parkes, "The Components of Reaction to Loss of a Limb, Spouse, or Home," *Journal of Psychosomatic Research* (16), pp. 343-49; and "Psychosocial

Transitions: Comparison Between Reactions to Loss of a Limb and Loss of a Spouse," *British Journal of Psychiatry* (127), pp. 204-10. Also Beverly Raphael, *The Anatomy of Bereavement* (New York: Basic Books, 1986), pp. 290ff.

11. See, for example, Joan Ablon, "Stigmatized Health Conditions," *Journal of Social Science and Medicine* 15B (1981), pp. 5-9. Ablon refers to the impact on general health of perceived loss of control over basic aspects of personal decision-making.

12. See Jan Cox-Gedmark, *Coping with Physical Disability* (Philadelphia: Westminster Press, 1980).

13. See chap. 1, note 4.

14. William E. Hulme, *Mid-Life Crises* (Philadelphia: Westminster Press, 1980), p. 13. Also Raphael, *Anatomy of Bereavement*, pp. 283ff.

15. Andrew D. Lester and Judith L. Lester, *Understanding Aging Parents* (Philadelphia: Westminster Press, 1980), p. 30.

16. J. Grayson, "Grief Reaction to the Relinquishing of Unfulfilled Wishes, *American Journal of Psychotherapy* 24 2 (1970), pp. 287-95.

17. John Bowlby, *Attachment and Loss, Vol. 3: Loss* (New York: Basic Books, 1980), p. 41.

18. Bowlby, *Loss*, p. 43.

19. "John and Mary Gibson" are not real people. The story is a composite derived from a number of family stories, and "John" and "Mary" and their children are merely representative of families who have undergone grief situations like those described. Neither are "Flint" and "Fort Myers" the locations of any of these stories, but represent the types of cultural shifts which families often face when forced by circumstances to relocate across country. Similarly, "First Church" does not refer to any specific congregation.

20. Yorick Spiegel, *The Grief Process: Analysis and Counseling* (Nashville: Abingdon Press, 1977), p. 80.

21. Glen Davidson, *Understanding Mourning* (Minneapolis: Augsburg Press, 1984), pp. 24-27.

22. Spiegel, *Grief Process*, p. 82.

23. Ibid., p. 82.

24. Rowan Gill, "Grief Is the Pain of Severed Love," *Church and Nation* (July 4, 1990).

25. Ronald H. Sunderland, *Working Through Your Grief* (Houston: SCI Inc., 1989), p. 15.

26. Spiegel, *Grief Process*, p. 101.

CHAPTER 4—Developing a Grief Ministry

1. Ronald H. Sunderland, "Lay Pastoral Care," *Primary Pastoral Care* (Atlanta: Editorial Board, *The Journal of Pastoral Care*, 1989).

2. The term *parish council* is used as a generic term to refer to any congregation's decision-making body having oversight over pastoral care and other ministries.

3. See Ronald H. Sunderland, "Children Talk About Grief," a 20-min. video presentation designed for parents to share with their children in the course of family grief education and response. It consists of three segments: the first five minutes is directed to children up to age of five or six years; the middle segment addresses concerns at the level of pre-teens; and the final segment speaks to adolescents. Thus, preschool children may view only the first segment, while adolescents may view the entire tape. The videotape is presented in the hope that it will assist families and church-school classes to address dying and death, and the anguish of grief openly and in a timely manner.

4. Alan Wolfelt, *A Child's View of Grief* (Houston: SCI Inc., 1990), p. 3.

5. These and other responses are addressed in *Caring About Kids: Talking to Children About Death* (U.S. Dept. of Health, Education, and Welfare, Publication, No. [ADM] 79-838, 1979). See also Earl A. Grollman, ed., *Explaining Death to Children* (Boston: Beacon Press, 1967).
6. Wolfelt, *Child's View of Grief*, p. 24.
7. Ibid., p. 27.
8. Wolfelt, "Chris," in "A Child's View of Grief," a 20-min. videotape in the SCI series, Sunderland, "Working Through Your Grief."

CHAPTER 5—Grief Support

1. Erich Lindemann, "Symptomatology and Management of Acute Grief," *American Journal of Psychiatry* (September 1944), p. 147.
2. Ibid.
3. Ibid.
4. Colin Murray Parkes, *Bereavement: Studies in Grief in Adult Life* (New York: International Universities Press, 1972), pp. 149-81.
5. Ibid., p. 175.
6. Ibid.
7. Ibid., p. 176. For a full account of this case, see Frances Beck, *Diary of a Widow: Rebuilding Family Life After the Funeral* (Boston: Beacon Press, 1965).
8. Parkes, *Bereavement*, p. 177.
9. J. William Worden, *Grief Counseling and Grief Therapy*, 2nd ed. (New York: Springer Publishing Co., 1991), p. 56.
10. Parkes, *Bereavement*, pp. 78ff.
11. Glen W. Davidson, *Understanding Mourning* (Minneapolis: Augsburg Publishing House, 1984).
12. Ibid., pp. 15-19.
13. Ibid., pp. 93.
14. Ibid., pp. 95-98.
15. Edwin Sneidman, *Survivors of Suicide*, ed. A. C. Cain (Springfield, Ill: Thomas, 1972). See also John Hewett, *After Suicide* (Philadelphia: Westminster Press, 1980), p. 117, for an extensive reading guide.
16. Worden, *Grief Counseling*, p. 81. It is not the intention of this book to provide detailed notes on specific topics such as murder or suicide. These are available in books such as that of Worden and other authors, to which readers should refer for more detailed coverage of these issues. My intention is to identify the special needs of survivors whose grief is intensified by trauma, in order to emphasize the point that, while most grieving survivors need continuing support in the months and years following the loved one's death, the deeper the perceived trauma, the greater the support that may be needed from caregivers.
17. See, for example, Erich Lindemann and I. M. Greek, "A Study of Grief: Emotional Responses to Suicide," *Pastoral Psychology* (November 4, 1953).
18. Beverly Raphael, *The Anatomy of Bereavement* (New York: Basic Books, 19183), p. 231.
19. See earlier note on the "Empty Nest Syndrome" in chap. 3.
20. Raphael, *Anatomy of Bereavement*, p. 276
21. Ibid., p. 262. Raphael's references are to the "Cornwell group": J. Cornwell, B. Nurcombe, and L. Stevens, "Family Response to Loss of a Child by Sudden Infant Death Syndrome," *Medical Journal of Australia* (April 30, 1977), pp. 656-58. See also J. Lowman, "Grief Intervention and Sudden Infant Death Syndrome," *American Journal of Community Psychology* 7 6, pp. 665-77.

22. Worden, *Grief Counseling*, p. 101.
23. Raphael, *Anatomy of Bereavement*, p. 270.
24. For example, see May and Breme, 1982, 1983, "SIDS Family Adjustment Scale: A Method of Assessing Family Adjustment in Sudden Infant Death Syndrome," *Omega* 13 1, pp. 59-74.
25. There is extensive literature related to the place of small groups in the life of the congregation, and to styles of leadership that are best suited to this task.
26. These suggestions were first presented in the booklet, *Establishing a Grief Support Group*, prepared as part of the SCI program, "Working Through Your Grief," the videotape which dramatizes a typical grief-support group session.

CHAPTER 6—Grief Education

1. Christopher Lasch, "Revaluing Political and Social Systems Toward a Usable Future," address to the 24th Annual Conference of the Association for Clinical Pastoral Education, Breckenridge, Col., November 20-24, 1991.
2. Donald Browning, "Pastoral Care and Public Ministry," *The Christian Century* (September 28, 1966), pp. 1175-77.
3. Ibid.
4. Ibid.
5. Earl A. Grollman, *Explaining Grief to Children* (Boston: Beacon Press, 1967), p. 4.
6. Fred Rogers, "Anything human is mentionable, and anything mentionable can be manageable," *The Director* (September 1991), p. 18.
7. Lawrence LeShan, Foreword, in Edgar Jackson, *Coping with the Crises in Your Life* (New York: Jason Aaronson, 1973), p. vii.
8. Jane E. Brody, "Better Conduct? Train Parents, Then Children," *The New York Times*, Science Times (December 3, 1991), p. B5.
9. Sam Keen, *Fire in the Belly* (New York: Bantam Books, 1991), pp. 134-36.
10. James B. Nelson, "The Moral Context of Counseling," *The Pastor as Counselor*, ed. Earl E. Shelp and Ronald H. Sunderland (New York: The Pilgrim Press, 1991), p. 62.
11. Personal communciation, October 24, 1991.
12. L. Joseph Stone et al., *Childhood and Adolescence* (New York: Random House, 1979), p. 338.
13. See, for example, John Bowlby, *Attachment and Loss, Vol. II: Separation* (New York: Basic Books, 1973), pp. 3-24; and *Vol. III: Loss* (New York: Basic Books, 1980), pp. 7-22.
14. Bowlby, *Loss*, p. 21.
15. Eda LeShan, *Learning to Say Good-bye* (New York: Avon Books, 1976, 1988), p. 23.
16. Ibid., p. 13.
17. Robert J. Kastenbaum, *Death, Society, and Human Experience*, 3rd ed. (Columbus, Ohio: Charles E. Merrill, 1986), p. viii.
18. Ibid., p. 257.
19. Donna O'Toole, *Growing Through Grief: A K-12 Curriculum to Help Young People Through All Kinds of Loss* (Burnsville, N.C.: Mountain Rainbow Publications, 1989), p. 6. The comprehensive and creative work of O'Toole and her associates is an invaluable tool for use in church- and day-school education. O'Toole provides teaching units that address the broad spectrum of content and modes of presentation for students K–12. Among the strengths of the curriculum are its integration of cognitive and affective aspects of grief and the insistence that allowing one to be in touch with and express feelings is a major factor in removing impediments to their expression.

20. Most groups will find that O'Toole's *Growing Through Grief* outlines and teaching aids more than meet their requirements for grades K–12.
21. Kastenbaum, *Death, Society, and Human Experience*, pp. 118-119.
22. Elizabeth Goss, "Living and Dying with AIDS," *The Journal of Pastoral Care* (Winter 1989), pp. 302, 304.
23. See, for example, Edgar N. Jackson, "Attitudes Toward Death in Our Culture," *Death and Bereavement*, ed. A. H. Kutscher (Springfield, Ill.: Charles C. Thomas, 1969), pp. 212-18.
24. Goss, "Living and Dying with AIDS," p. 305.
25. Ibid.
26. Ronald H. Sunderland, "Caring for People Living and Dying with AIDS," *The Journal of Pastoral Care* (Winter 1989), p. 312.